# HER VOICE

FINDING YOURSELF

*For all the women who are on the journey to finding themselves. We hope these words will help show you the way.*

# CONTENTS

## 1

# LEARNING TO BE ON MY OWN

SANGRIA SISTERS

"Three to five months." The words spilled out of the oncologist's mouth, and time stood still. Despite the cloudy daze, I heard the words with somber clarity. While the rest of the world moved on, our worst case scenario became a harsh reality. We get that we're all on borrowed time, but the finality of these words was devastating.

Diagnosed with Stage 4 terminal cancer, my husband Scott was handed his expiry date. There was so much to do and so little time to do it, including a plethora of appointments to attend, care to give, a house to run, a daughter to protect, family and friends to keep connected, and a dog to love. After 26 years together, the whole thing was a mind fuck.

There's no time to think about yourself or how this will affect you. Years ago, a therapist diagnosed me as co-dependent, and at that time the prospect of flying solo would have sent me into a tailspin. I had to learn to take control of the cockpit to prevent my mental health from a crash and burn.

I'd lost my Dad to cancer three years earlier, and didn't have the tools to handle the stress. I turned to antidepressants for stability. I had to try on numerous "glass slippers" to find the right Rx fit. I'd never felt more unlike myself, but this round I was determined to get through the tragedy without a repeat crash landing. This time I came prepared.

As the baby of the family, I prefer to have things done for me. In my 20's, I had all the cockiness of a bird who flew from my parent's nest straight into my sister's basement. By my 30's, I was a busy stay-at-home mom, all the while losing my identity, and dependent on a husband who was now a full-fledged alcoholic.

The 40's were thankfully a gentler decade. Scott stopped drinking cold turkey, and I became a kinder, less cynical person. My daughter Abby was more independent, I was thriving in my job, but I was still critical of myself. I still couldn't trust that I had value. All it took were two tragic events to show me what I was made of.

I had to recognize that this was Scott's journey and I was merely the co-pilot. I wasn't the one dying, and by no means was I all alone. Family and friends stepped up and stepped in. I have an amazing tribe, but eventually everyone has their own life to attend to. When all is quiet, you stand up and rebuild, or lie down and turtle. It is most definitely a choice.

On Saturday, October 27, 2018, Scott passed away.

In my mind, the absolute worst was going to happen now that I was alone. I mourned the loss of my husband AND my life as I knew it. But time and experience have led me to my mid 50's, and a place of self-serenity I didn't see coming. I am eternally grateful for my army of angels working overtime to provide me with faith, hope and love.

I was quickly introduced to the fucking "blue" jobs. The shit work women don't want to do. One thing after another needed repair and attention. Trouble comes in threes, so you need to learn how to isolate them one at a time. Banking, money, house repairs, yard work, taxes, car maintenance, garbage, snaking the drain. You name it, I *now* know how to do it. As a list girl, check marking chores is satisfying AF. With every task mastered there is a growing empowerment.

At some point, I'll prepare the family home for sale. Clean it out, fix it up, widdle it down. The legalities and listing it all on my own are big shoes for a co-dependent to fill. Thank goodness for YouTube. You can google a virtual husband to answer life's questions without him trying to fix it. And he can be muted! The real life people you want to surround yourself with are your 'sistahs.' Together you can do anything...or know a guy who can.

My priorities have become crystal clear. Taking ownership of my life, I've graduated from flight simulator to top gun pilot. *My* house, *my* car, *my* yard, *our* daughter. I'm learning to differentiate different kinds of stress. Is it a big thing, or not worth the anxiety?

What's life like now? I do what I love to do. I listen to music, dance, grow out all my body hair, and eat the whole pizza. I can finally say I'm happy without feeling guilty. I've got a crush on the girl in the mirror. I'd hang with her. She's the one who's determined to live up to her potential, a little tardy, but perfectly on time for her next chapter.

I highly recommend asserting independence by living on your own, before you find a (room) mate. You have experience to draw on, and it helps with the learning curve. Life is one big journey with a series of adventures and opportunities for growth. Uncharted waters with unlimited horizons are my next destination. Staying present helps me stay grounded, so when opportunity knocks, I'll be ready for takeoff.

Watch me soar with the birds and shine like the stars!

2

## MISS SELF-RELIANT

SHELBY WATT

"Nothing can bring you peace but yourself." -Ralph Waldo Emerson

I need to preface by stating how wildly cliché I feel submitting a coming of age, non-fiction story about a twenty-something year old woman, whose boy troubles were the catalyst to a journey of self-discovery she could compare only to that of Eat, Pray, Love. But regardless, it does sound interesting, don't you think?

My name is Shelby. I work in the oilfield in Alberta, Canada, and I fit almost every stereotype you could think of, in only the best ways, though. I've spent most of my adult life chasing money across the province, picking up some questionable habits, and suffering from a serious case of work/life imbalance. I was raised by a pipeliner, and a single mother who was also raised by a pipeliner and a single mother. It must be hereditary. One thing is abundantly clear; I was led by example, and taught how to pack up when the going got going. But you and I haven't found each other only to go over my family lineage. Maybe we can visit that another time. For now, I'll attempt to summarize my most profound period of self-discovery in 2,500 words or less!

I broke up with someone a couple of years back. It still feels weird saying that because for a hot-minute I thought I'd be married to him by now. Somehow, it's two years later and I'm the most single I've ever been, but much to my surprise, I'm the happiest I've ever been as well. I'll spare you the gory details, but at the time it felt like I magically fell out of love with my soul mate. I felt that I'd just magically woken up one morning and my heart had frozen over. Remaining, was an impenetrable ice block, never to bleed for that boy again. So, in May of 2019 we broke up, and it took until September 2020 for me to fully understand it.

Hi, I'm Shelby, and I'm a recovering co-dependent. What an interesting concept *that* was to reflect on.

I semi recently spent a couple of weeks attached at the hip to a new romantic fixation that I'm not totally convinced isn't the father of my future children... but um... he like, doesn't love me? And, when I say I cannot compute that, I mean it. This one is, for all intents and purposes, the actual man of my dreams. I built him in my head as a child, and he manifested right before my very eyes on some sour gas lease in central Alberta. He's 6'2, with luscious black hair, great teeth, a full moustache, big hands, sexy tattoos, brown eyes, and biceps. Google the realistic painted depiction of Prince Eric. He could have modelled for that photo. And, do not get me started on who he is as a person. Okay fine, I'll tell you. He is successful, intelligent, hardworking, well-respected, athletic, quick witted, confident, compassionate (although, he would never admit it), and on and on and on. For real, ask my friends, I can go on forever. He's really great. Somehow though, all of *that* isn't overly interested in all of *this,* and I was desperately beating my head off the wall trying to figure out why – until now.

You see, a sneaky pattern I have is falling in love as a distraction from myself. This is something I didn't notice, because I've always *loved* myself. There have been things, such as body image, lifestyle, and comparison, that I haven't always adored. But, for the most part *me* and *I* have been pretty good friends... or, so I thought. You see, I was able to maintain that inner peace because I had boyfriends to validate how I felt about myself. \*\*Insert previously mentioned ex-boyfriend who I tricked into falling in love with me by pretending I was super happy with the bare minimum and being the 'cool-girl/best-girl-ever' because I needed him to love me in order to prove to myself that I was loveable. All the while however, I was letting resentments and micro-aggressions build up so greatly that I could no longer stand the sight of him.\*\*

I wasn't able to see it that way at the time though, because I've been historically independent. I don't need anyone, for anything. I know, right? Trauma. It's that 'single mother' type mother wound. Ah, therapy! For me, 'co-dependency' and 'I can't support myself and need everyone/anyone else to take care of me' were synonymous, so I never looked into it. I'm also a serial monogamist, meaning I'd been single for approximately 5 minutes since I was 16 years old. *Imagine* the unturned stones of my identity that I've been uncovering over the last two years. *Imagine* how frantically I leached onto Prince Eric so that I didn't have to face the unknown territory of self. *Imagine* why he literally kissed me, and then washed his hands of my needy ass. He knew then (probably on a subconscious level) what I know now, which is that as independent as I thought I was, I needed him to think the world of me in order to think the world of myself. And that's a lot of extra responsibility to take on when you're a grown up, lovely, wonderful, and sexy man. It's too much to ask of anyone else, and so began the rest of my life.

This shiny new chapter began with a shiny new journal. I've

dabbled in journaling all my life. I love to write and I love to talk about myself and how wise I am, so this practice was relatively seamless for me. The only exception was that I had a lot of shit talking to get out of my system before I could meet myself compassionately. I recently read the first page I'd written back in October, and it was a treacherous mind-dump of a very sad 26-year-old who could not stop calling herself an idiot to save her life. It was actually hard to read because I don't feel that way about myself or even that version of myself at all anymore. Thank goodness. I read on, and saw how I spent days in a slump of, 'He's not into me, and here are the 500 ways I agree with him that I'm not good enough.' What a trap. Maybe you've been there too, where you find yourself face-to-face with rejection and it triggers all your deep-seeded self-rejection, and now not only do you *not* get the guy, but you're stuck being this person that *he* doesn't like. And off he goes, getting to fully experience his own excellence at all times, leaving you in the sewer to stink. That's how my co-dependency feels. If I can please you, I'm pleased. If I can't, I'm worthless.

I'm happy to report that the pages have become far less self-deprecating. I read Emerson's Self-Reliance. Correction, I read the spark notes. Old English is not for me. I came to understand how much of my life, romantically and otherwise, is dependent on someone else's input.

Am I making the right choice? Call Mom.

Should I buy a new car? Call Dad.

Am I worthy of affection, love, and happiness? Call Prince Eric.

I realized that I wasn't using input from other people as a soundboard, but rather to completely alleviate any or all responsibility for my life and where it's headed. Again, totally unbeknownst to me, because I'm *so* independent, remember?

I had no idea who I was without consulting everyone else.

The more I looked around, the more aware I became of just how little of my life *I'd* intentionally created, and how much of it had been handed down to me. All of the "if I were yous" and "maybe you shoulds" echoed across my basement suite, and into my mind. It scared me. It still does, because it means that anything I feel might be *off* or *out of alignment* is ultimately up to me to change. And that means changing a lot in ways that my co-creators might not be comfortable with, and then having to take responsibility for any consequences of my own choices? Big yikes.

Needless to say, I've chosen the word 'trust' for the year 2021 in lieu of a resolution. I feel like I've really met myself in ways I wasn't comfortable with before. I now notice the difference between asking for guidance from others, and needing someone else to take the wheel because I don't know what's best for me. "What should I do?" is now a question I reserve only for myself. "What would you do?" is a tool I reserve exclusively for folks I deeply respect, but it's never the default solution to my problem.

I'm slowly learning that discomfort doesn't always mean sudden death; and disapproval doesn't always mean I'm doing it wrong. Rejection doesn't mean I'm not exceptionally incredible. I am, at all times, the most powerful person in my experience. There have been people, or situations that have challenged that idea, but I know better now. I'm my safest bet. I worked my ass off to believe it, but truthfully, I've been here the whole time. Perhaps the loudest realization in all of this, is that Prince Eric wasn't the one that got away. It was never about him. I was the one who was using the poor boy to run away from myself. It took some teary nights, staring in the mirror and sitting in my desperate loneliness to finally come to terms with my projection of what loneliness means. But, once I'd faced it and re-learned to enjoy my own company, I could finally find peace in the exceptional alright-ness of not having someone to hold my hand. There lies all of the power. Power that was never lost, only forgotten. And it's never to be forgotten again.

# 3

# MAEKING IT HAPPEN

MAE KROEIS

I followed the path most of us do. You know, the one our parents encourage us to follow that's supposed to lead to life-long happiness?

It goes like this:

Do well in high school. Get into a good post-secondary school. Choose a sensible program of study. Get a Master's degree if you're smart, and/or get a job right out of school that pays well enough to decrease debt and start saving ASAP. Stay at that job, even if you don't really like it, because you get good benefits and your employer matches your pension contributions. Suck up, and try to get promoted.

So, that's what I did.

And when I completed the last of those steps on that prescribed path to happiness, I started to panic.

Was this really all there was to life? Aside from weekend adventures and hobbies to fill my free time, was this what life was all about? Was this all I had to look forward to for the next 60 years?

I couldn't bear to think that the mundane routine of heading to the office 5 days out of 7 and sitting at my computer was all I had to look forward to for the next 40 years.

There had to be something missing but I had no idea what that *something* was.

I thought maybe my problem was the job so I switched a few times. With each job change, I did feel a renewed sense of purpose but that feeling always faded and I would find myself right back to where I was before: restless, purposeless, and like I was wasting my potential and watching my life pass me by.

In the meantime, I had followed the other half of that prescribed path to happiness that involved finding a partner and "settling down".

At 28 I got pregnant and I was thrilled about my upcoming maternity leave. It would be like a vacation, a break from the mundane routine of the office, a time to do what I wanted, and a chance to rediscover what I might truly want for my life.

But, like any mom knows, maternity leave is not a vacation, and when my twelve months of it was up, back to work I went, feeling more desperate and less sure about the meaning of life. I had even less time now to explore interests and potential alternative careers. The increase in my responsibility meant I couldn't easily now walk away from my dependable well-paying job to pursue something new (or so I thought at the time).

The next year was a tough adjustment. My partner worked construction with long hours, and I worked full-time. Raising a family with two full-time working parents was stressful and busy. I didn't want to be at work five days a week. I wanted to spend more time with my daughter, and I wanted more time for myself. But, ultimately, I couldn't afford to be off work.

I got pregnant again when my daughter was just over a year old and went for the first viability ultrasound at nine weeks. The technicians were awkward and kept questioning my dates. Then, the doctor came in and told me that the embryo was measuring six weeks, with no heartbeat. It was a 'missed miscarriage'.

A missed miscarriage is when your body *misses* the fact that the would-be baby in your body stopped growing. It's like it forgets, or hasn't yet clued into the fact, that things aren't going according to plan inside your uterus.

My body had already gone 3 weeks without clueing in.

And I was supposed to go to Vegas with my sister that weekend for my mom's surprise 60th birthday.

My doctor said my body would eventually realize it needed to miscarry, so she encouraged me to go on my trip regardless and gave me some general guidelines on what to expect and when to go to the hospital should that become necessary.

I went to Vegas hoping the miscarriage, whenever it happened, would be like what I had read on blogs: like a heavy period. And initially, that is how it started, but the bleeding worsened fast and didn't stop.

While going through it, I wasn't thinking clearly about whether I needed to go to the hospital. I obviously had reservations about going to an emergency room in another country. I couldn't tell if the bleeding was bad enough to warrant a hospital visit, or if what I was experiencing was normal. I didn't want to go all the way to the hospital (bleeding through my maxi pads and my pants) only to sit in a waiting room and get turned away.

My mom, sister and I debated back and forth. I told myself I was feeling the same as when I donated blood: not comfortable, but okay.

Until all of a sudden, I wasn't okay. I nearly passed out on the toilet and had to lay down on the bathroom floor as the blood loss finally caught up to me. I realized we were past the point of going to the ER. I couldn't move, let alone put underwear on. We needed an ambulance.

I was scared. The situation had escalated and I felt like an idiot for not doing something sooner.

While we waited anxiously for the ambulance to arrive, I went into shock from blood loss. One of my feet started to feel numb, and then my leg, hip, torso and neck. As my tongue became fat and heavy, and my throat closed, I told my mom to tell my partner and daughter I loved them. In that moment, I truly thought I might die.

The paramedics arrived moments later and luckily, the numbness faded and I was taken to the hospital.

My experience there was traumatic. I clung to the brief moments of kindness from a few of the staff but it took Eye Movement Desensitization and Reprocessing (EMDR) therapy to ease the other memories. I had an emergency dilation and curettage (D&C) operation and a blood transfusion.

When I finally got home, I was severely anemic, which seemed to be the worst of my symptoms considering both the physical and mental.

I didn't take much time off work. I wanted life to feel normal. I didn't relate to the grief I had heard other moms feel in response to losing a pregnancy. I just had some trauma to process and some anemia to recover from.

We did want another child though. So, we waited three months, as doctors recommend after a miscarriage, and tried again. I was so nervous for that first viability ultrasound, and couldn't believe it when the technicians, yet again, told me there was no heartbeat. Two embryonic sacs, no embryos.

How could this happen twice?

This time, my doctor referred me to the early loss clinic where they could schedule surgery for the missed miscarriage. But there was a wait to be seen for an intake appointment and it was a long weekend. I was terrified I'd end up in the ER before I could get the surgery I needed or even an initial appointment.

In the end, as I had worried, the scheduled D&C wasn't going to be for another couple of weeks. This meant I would be waiting a total of one month from the time I first discovered the failed pregnancy, to the D&C.

I spent this next month terrified I would hemorrhage at any moment. Sure enough, in the early hours of the day my operation was scheduled, the cramping began. We knew right away it was an emergency situation.

The second time around, at the hospital, was slightly more comforting knowing I was home in Calgary. I did need an emergency D & C (thankfully no blood transfusion) but I had still lost a lot of blood and been poked and prodded enough to re-traumatize me.

After this second emergency operation, I was completely destroyed. The trauma and blood loss were too much. Even though I still didn't feel sad about a lost infant, I decided to access the free grief counselling offered through the early loss clinic.

During therapy, the counsellor explained that sometimes our bodies store memories too. She invited me to find out what my body had to say about my experience, and what it thought I needed in order to heal.

As I turned inward, I saw an image of myself trying to hold onto a golden light. In my meditation, I understood that this light was the Universe's energy and that rather than trying to hold onto it for myself (i.e. trying to keep a baby) I could let it go because this energy was already in the world all around me.

The message I understood from this vision was that we cannot hold on too tightly to anything in this world. If we release the need to have ultimate control over our lives, and instead follow what feels right and true, we will be led in the direction that is right for us.

I took this message to heart and walked away with a completely new perspective on my situation and on life.

This mindset shift was the beginning of my new path to a more fulfilling, purposeful life. I continued to tune into the energy of the Universe as I healed mentally and physically from my experiences. Moving forward, anytime I started to feel down on myself or sad or wistful, I remembered the golden light's presence all around me.

After this transcendent experience, I couldn't bear the thought of going back to my cubicle and spending day after day bored and unfulfilled. I wanted my whole life to feel different. I didn't need to change everything but I wanted *more*.

I wanted to feel inspired. I wanted to spend my days doing something meaningful where I was using my strengths and living to my full potential.

It was time to find my true purpose: what was I really meant to be doing with my life?

I dug deep. I reflected. I read. I took more time off work. I slowed down.

One of the books I read suggested asking friends what they would most likely turn to you for help with, and it was this question that first got me thinking about life coaching.

I realized that what most lit me up was empowering others, supporting them, relating to them, offering tools to help, and translating research into tangible advice. I already had a wealth of knowledge in mental health and positive psychology from my academic and professional background so the idea of combining this with professional coaching skills and entrepreneurship was exciting.

Maybe this was the *more* I had been searching for.

Even though I had reservations and doubts, I went for it and through my coach training, learned a lot about how to support others through their own limiting beliefs around pursuing new paths.

I became a life coach. I got pregnant again, and I now get to hear the heartbeat inside my son's chest anytime I want. I quit my job and found a great, flexible, part-time one. I started Maek it Happen Life Coaching where I specialize in helping people who feel stuck, at work or in their lives, figure out what they're really meant to be doing and 'maek' it happen.

It lights me up to help others live more fulfilling lives. I understand why people stay in comfortable but miserable situations; but, I hold hope for each one of my clients, believing that they will find the *more* they're looking for.

Don't stick it out in a soul sucking job for the pension, or insist that it's too risky to make a change. Don't settle for what you already have instead of wanting more because you think you should be more grateful. Life is meant to *live*. Don't wait for burn out, old age or something terrible to happen to convince you to make a change. If you need a helping hand to guide you towards a new path, I'm here for you 'maeking' my *it* happen too.

# 4

## FITNESS MOM
TANYA BAST

Being a fitness competitor was the biggest and best challenge of my life, so I thought. It takes the power of the mind and the body to achieve something that most people won't even try. It involved putting myself out of my comfort zone both physically and mentally. It also required years of committing myself solely to "me," and dedicating my life to my hobby in order to build my career as a trainer. I missed so many events to train, diet, and ensure that I was not tempted. I would skip holiday meals so that my specific menu wasn't a burden on anyone. Some people understood, and others were taken aback by this whole commitment I had taken on. And this was not once; I took stage nine times not counting numerous photoshoot and events. I always felt I needed to improve each time, which is common with any sport. It truly was a love /hate relationship.

After years of loving this, I started to dislike it. I wanted it all to go away. Towards the end I was suffering and exhausted. I didn't want be selfish anymore. I wanted more from life, not just the perfection of my body. I wanted a life much different than the one I was currently living. It was like I was isolating myself from everything. It wasn't all the glitz and glam it looked like. It was hard.

By this time, when I hung up my competition heels, I wanted a family. I thought having a baby may also help take away my addiction to being perfect. Perhaps putting it all behind me would lead to caring for more than just my own body's perfection. After quitting competitions, dieting, and the photo shoots, it took some time to recover from my changing body. The competition look is just not sustainable. In fact, in can be dangerously unhealthy; but, with my knowledge and expertise as a coach and trainer I helped myself become acceptant of my new body and embrace the life I envisioned for the future. There were still challenging moments, but it felt good to finally be "normal."

I became pregnant on the first try. I knew I was in a good place. I never felt better in my body. I was balanced, healthy, glowing and tight. I loved every bit of the experience, and was pleasantly surprised that all the horror stories I had heard did not come true for me. I celebrated my strong body. Perhaps all my fitness struggles paid off in the way I loved to be pregnant. I embraced the ability of my body to grow a baby, and perhaps my comfort with the experience was just related to where I was in this chapter of my life. I was exactly where I wanted to be. I felt good.

Once I became a mom, it wasn't about me anymore; it was about nurturing a tiny human who I fell madly in love with while taking care of, and loving every aspect of myself through the process. That's what I wanted. I didn't need perfection anymore, just balance and a whole tool belt full of new life tools.

Even as a professional trainer, it's tough to fit workouts in daily. I honestly don't have the time, strength, or extreme motivation I had. *This is so not me*, I thought to myself. *You find the time, strength, and motivation for things you're passionate about.*

Had I lost that passion, or was it just not my first priority anymore? That was it, it just wasn't my first priority anymore. In fact, workouts were on the back-burner now. I found different activities to do that included my daughter, like walking, running and quick home workouts with cartoons in the back ground. No, it isn't the same, but it's refreshing.

I now have a different outlook on life, fitness, health, happiness and balance. I feel more centred and driven to try new things.

For many years, I was solely dedicated to myself and it taught me that perfection is not reality. On the positive side though, it taught me willpower, patience and to believe that I can conquer anything I set my mind to.

Now, as a mom, I'm dedicated, patient, strong, beautiful, and motivated, but in a different way. And, that's perfect for me. I accomplish more things in a day with a toddler than I thought possible. I often call myself 'mom of the year' and for me that reward is the motivation to make me a better person every day. Priorities shift as life evolves. In fact, everything shifts. That doesn't make you less motivated, determined or strong. It makes you human, and with that, there is growth and an opportunity for new adventures.

Life is an ongoing search of discovering ourselves; each day, each year, each decade, you will have an opportunity to create a great story.

# 5

# THE HEART OF INDIA
PHILIPPA KAYE

Back in 1998 I made my first trip to India. I had been asked by three investors to set up a travel company for them. They had decided on South India, and I was despatched to Recce with the aim of determining the product, then, writing the brochure and launching the company. The initial plan was that I would spend three weeks, inspecting hotels and places to visit. It soon became apparent that three weeks wouldn't be long enough to cover the three southern states of Kerala, Tamil Nadu and Karnataka. Three weeks became six. Now, I did enjoy my travels, and was determined to get away from where I was expected to go in order to find a few good hotels. But, there were a lot of bad ones, with lackadaisical service at best. Additionally, I didn't have an understanding of India at the time. My guides weren't great, and it seemed that at every site and temple I was taken to, I was viewed merely as a meal ticket: Go here, get a blessing and donate to the priest. Kids wanted money; widows wanted money; and I was instructed repeatedly to go into shops and buy things. Now, don't get me wrong, I liked the good hotels, and was amazed at the temples. My first backwaters experience on a houseboat blew me away. But, after five weeks on the road viewing temples, and being stared at and begged at: I wasn't feeling the love. I liked India, but I couldn't appreciate why people fell in love with it.

I happened to get talking to Manoj, the receptionist at a hotel, and told him that I just wanted to see an India where I didn't get viewed as a meal ticket, or have to look at a building. He immediately invited me to his home village 30 kilometres away and the following day, we went. Now, for the life of me, I can't remember where it was, but the experience has stuck with me through all of these years.

The first people I saw were three ladies, sitting on a veranda. Their faces were covered with a yellow paste. They smiled at me and put their hands together in a traditional Namaste, seemingly unaware of how strange they actually looked. Manoj told me they had covered their faces with a mixture of sandalwood and turmeric: sandalwood for its cooling properties, and turmeric for its anti-ageing benefits, basically a traditional sunscreen.

Around the corner there were two women sitting on another large step. One lady, probably in her eighties, was wrinkled and wizened, yet with kind eyes and a gentle demeanour. She was looking at a collection of small shells, scattered on the floor. The other, much younger lady, was looking at her intently, and gently weeping. I had stumbled across the village wise woman or soothsayer who told fortunes with a combination of etched palm leaves and sea-shells. The younger woman's son had died, which would be devastating to begin with, but a child dying in *this* village was considered to be the result of a curse on the family. The younger woman had sought the investigative services of the soothsayer and was seeking a path to redemption.

By this time, I had gathered an audience: a bunch of barefooted children who were literally jumping up and down, shrieking and giggling with uncontrollable excitement. It was impossible not to be caught up in their ho. Shy girls would peek out from behind older siblings, and the braver boys would run up to me, shriek "One photo," and then run away again. I looked around to seek out their parents to ask permission, and a nearby adult waved vaguely and indicated that I could go ahead. This was long before the days of the smart phone, when photography was still done with a camera. And, in such a remote village, this was a rare opportunity that I didn't want to miss. Soon, other children arrived, and their mothers appeared, smiling shyly but delighted for such a disturbance from their everyday routine.

After much posing and demands for more, one brave lady who had been watching from the side lines came up and gently touched my skin. She looked up and caught my eye, concern in hers, "Paining?" she asked. They had never seen freckles before. It was that moment that I experienced a dawning: a realization that as a traveller, we are as much of an oddity to the people in the places we visit as they are to us.

Taking her cue from her mother, a girl came up and touched my hair. Auburn isn't a familiar colour for them. I squatted down and let them stroke my hair and my skin. Before long I was being pawed by seven or eight of them. Attracted by the noise, more people started coming out of their houses. The children were batted away and in the next instant I was invited into a home. Now this wasn't a wealthy village by any stretch of the imagination, but this was to be my first experience of true, genuine Indian hospitality, where 'Guest is God.'

I was shown around this simple home by the lady of the house, as well as her sister, mother and aunt. It was no more really than one room with a courtyard and a veranda out front. A couple of charpois were the entirety of the furniture, and there was a rudimentary kitchen area. They offered me water, and then buttermilk fresh from the cooler, but there were no fridges. I was torn between getting ill and insulting these wonderfully kind ladies, who had very little but wanted to give me what they could. I took the plunge, sipped at the water and drank the buttermilk. They were delighted, a fact given away by the broadest, most brilliant smiles I had ever seen. A conversation then ensued, purely in sign language, about families, numbers of children and whether they were boys and girls. As I left, I asked Manoj the local word for thank you, and repeated it to these ladies. They wouldn't hear of it; no thanks were necessary. I was a guest, and their home was my home.

Word spread further and the man from the street food stall sent me some of his snacks to try. Then, having finished with her client, the village wise woman asked me if I wanted to have my fortune told. Why not? I settled down on her step while a very large crowd watched over, to see what lay in store. No one would take a rupee for any of this. In fact, I was told it was insulting of me to offer. By the end of my two hours there, I was captivated. And, I realized that the true India is shown by the hearts of its people.

This is the one key memory that remained with me from that whole trip. It was a catalytic moment, although it took a few years for me to realize it. You see, over the next few years, I was dragged around the mainstream destinations, to see the must-see monuments and was harassed by the touts. But, at the back of my mind, this memory was always there, niggling away at me. Eight years later, I had the opportunity to run a lodge in a tiger reserve, and I spent as much time exploring the villages and meeting the locals as I did in search of wildlife in the national park. I then stayed in India to live for over a decade, knowing that there is so much more to the country than most people even realize. I used this knowledge as an opportunity, and I broke away from the mainstream tourism circuits and searched for the true India; the India behind the history and its monuments. I met the people, and did what the locals did. I explored things off the beaten track, whether by car, foot, horse, camel or jeep. I visited the old towns, villages and places that most people have never heard of. I learned about the culture of India's people and their family values. And ultimately, because of its people, I fell in love with the country.

India is a magical place. Her people are some of the most humble, hospitable, resilient and enterprising folk in the world. In the cities it is very different, but in the rural communities, one comes to realize that it isn't the possessions that one has that makes a person. Rather, it is what's in their hearts; and this has stuck with me ever since that first visit. As my father said, after his first visit to the country at almost 80 years old: "There are so many people who may not have much materially, but who have huge smiles, humbling hospitality, and a sense of joy."

This was the slow burning, life changing lesson that my first visit to that village taught me.

# 6

# STEELY RESOLVE
## BY PIXIE WRIGHT

I was forty years old when the last piece of the puzzle fell into place. It was not dramatic. You'd think that the final death of a turbulent marriage would conjure up some panic. Nope, not for me. I'm not one to panic. After all, I was raised in a rough and tumble family full of adrenaline junkies. I watched my father compete in death defying rodeo events my entire childhood, while some of his cowboy friends lost their lives in front of our eyes. You don't grow up in that environment without it changing your ability to handle adversity. I have guts of steel. I learned early on how to numb the scariness of life. As a result, I struggled as an adult to protect myself emotionally. Even if calling it quits on a toxic relationship meant emotional survival, you'd usually find me hanging on tight. You see, I wasn't exactly in denial about my marriage. I just refused to jump ship until the last possible second. Divorce was for the weak, didn't you know? Or so I had been conditioned to believe.

Because of this, I minimized my husband's drug and alcohol habit. I ignored his mental breakdowns. I hunkered down and refused to allow it all to get to me. My kids and I would be fine. I was a highly competent mother. My own father had nothing to do with me and so my kids could make it with an absentee dad, I rationalized. I never needed my husband to help me parent. As long as I kept him on the periphery of our daily lives, my kids and I could manage.

The first time he threatened suicide, my youngest daughter was a year old. I was shocked, terrified, and extremely confused. For me, his threats always seemed to come out of the blue, because his state did not jive with what was happening in our lives. There truly was no sense to be made however, because my husband's outbursts were fueled by amphetamines, alcohol and painkillers. It would take me years to understand that in threatening to end his life, he was manipulating me in an attempt to control the situation.

I begged him to get psychological help each time he made the threats. He did not. Years later, a good friend provided sage advice when I expressed my ongoing fear that he would commit suicide. She said, "It's not the ones who threaten in the heat of the moment that you have to worry about." Perhaps this is true, but It didn't stop me from worrying that he would take his life and do permanent emotional damage to our children in the process.

When he would go into a suicidal rant, I focused on how to keep my children from hearing it. I would purposely move away from their bedrooms so they couldn't hear him. Since he loved to "work" at our family business, I often encouraged him to leave. It turns out that being a workaholic isn't that far from being a drug addict. It wasn't that I didn't care about him, it was that my children took precedence. Each time he drove out of the driveway over those last few years, I breathed a sigh of relief. It was much easier to give them stability when he was gone.

I began discovering the unmarked pill bottles first in his bathroom, then in his truck, and then in his tool box. I always questioned him, and it always led to a fight. Nothing was ever resolved. He refused to admit that he had a problem, claimed he had prescriptions, and always circled back around to his favourite excuse. It was all my fault. You see, I was so demanding that he had to work nonstop to keep up financially. If he was abusing drugs to work all hours, I was to blame.

Funnily enough, the day he drove home in his brand new $100,000.00 Porsche, which he purchased without my knowledge using cash from our business, it for once had nothing to do with me. My husband was not only addicted to drugs, he was addicted to a flashy lifestyle as well. But all that glitters, is not gold. Unfortunately, my marriage taught me much more than I ever wanted to know about the connection between fast cars and fast pills, not to mention fast women. There were plenty of those too. I just chose to look the other way.

There was the hair transplant surgery. My husband was bald when we met. I loved him that way, but it didn't matter. He announced to me late one night that he was having the procedure the next morning. It involved him travelling five hours and having his scalp cut open from ear to ear. There was no discussion. It was already arranged, and how dare I even question something he wanted to do for himself. He worked so hard for our family after all.

When I found out the procedure cost $40,000.00, I was furious. There were several months that I could barely afford groceries on the living allowance he provided from our business. However, I knew that there was no point in addressing my anger with him. For the record, he looked better bald.

He began losing weight rapidly, claiming that he was trying to. He told me that losing weight made him feel so much better. His job was physical after all and he had endured back surgery once. It was better for his joints to carry less body weight. I found the drastic change in his appearance sickening, to be honest. It turns out amphetamines are a damn effective weight loss tool. You just have to be able to handle the mental instability.

Then there was the dinner party we attended where my husband entertained the guests with stories of the wonderful new drug he had discovered. He claimed that it gave him so much energy he could work nonstop, and wasn't that fantastic? A few couples rode home together with a designated driver that night. In the back seat of the car, my tipsy friend whispered about the stories my husband had been sharing. Awkward.

Somehow, none of those things, or even the culmination of all of those things, was quite enough to make me wake up and face reality. Never one to wave the white flag, I stood fast in my belief that I could do enough alone to keep it all together.

And then one day, the year I turned forty, my 'ah-ha' moment arrived.

The final puzzle piece fell into place.

And, get this. It came in the form of an old friend named Steely Resolve.

Steely Resolve appeared before me during our last family vacation. The destination was odd for a family trip, but years earlier my husband had declared that Las Vegas was the only place he'd ever felt truly happy. I should have known then. This particular vacation would prove to be doubling as his latest withdrawal episode off of whatever drug he'd been shoving down his throat or up his nose, as of late.

About a week before we left to go, he once again got mysteriously sick. His night sweats were so severe I had to throw out his pillows. I could not get the smell out in the wash. He developed a terrible cough. Once again, he began to threaten suicide. I suggested he go to the emergency room. But when he got there, for some reason, the doctors wouldn't give him anything to treat his condition. Hmmm. The day of our departure, I packed up all of the suitcases and piled everything and everyone into the truck. I made the five hour drive to the airport hotel, and my children and I suffered through another sleepless night while my husband paced, coughed, sweated profusely, and jonesed for whatever drug he was coming off of at the time.

By the time we settled in to the Grand Desert Resort in Las Vegas, we had been in and out of pharmacies for days searching for something to help my husband. On day three, and on the advice of my husband's physician back in Canada, I determined that he should go to the nurse practitioner at a Walgreens pharmacy close to the resort. I put on my heaviest armour for this battle and proceeded to drag my poor children and my husband to Walgreens.

We waited for what seemed like eternity. My husband had the shivers so I bought him a blanket to sit with while he waited. The children and I went for a walk in the sun and ordered some milkshakes at Sonic a few blocks away, which my girls loved. I always did try to keep things as light as possible for them in those days. I did that for a long time, until the perfect family story just wasn't in the cards anymore.

When we returned to Walgreens, he was in the treatment room being assessed. What came next would officially change the trajectory of our marriage forever, although I didn't know it at the time. The nurse began taking his blood pressure, and I was shocked when she looked up at me and said, "We need to call an ambulance."

I immediately went into problem solver mode, trying to keep my girls from being scared by this. They were always my first priority. I quickly busied them with something outside the nurse's room and then closed the door to begin asking the hard questions. "How much might it cost for Canadians vacationing in the United States to call an ambulance? Can I drive him to the hospital myself, and where is the nearest one?"

The nurse insisted that my husband's blood pressure was

dangerously low and she didn't recommend driving him to the hospital. Inside, I raged at his immaturity and lack of responsibility for doing this to all of us. What a pathetic excuse for a husband and father. I silently fumed. Did this make me a bad person? Or just plain fed up? I still don't know the answer.

Minutes later, the paramedics arrived. My girls were so scared. I don't think I'll ever forgive him for that. They assessed my husband and a paramedic pulled me aside to say, "This will cost you thousands of dollars. He is sick, but not in severe distress. You should drive him yourself to the Valley Hospital Medical Centre." So, in conclusion, nurse practitioner says one thing and paramedic lady says another. Great. Awesome. Perfect.

At that moment, I looked at my husband in his pathetic state and hated him with the heat of a thousand suns. I found everything about him in that situation abhorrent. How could he allow himself to get to this point? The resentment I harboured over our fifteen year relationship was threatening to boil over.

I felt fifteen years worth of anger rising from my toes all the way up to the top of my skull. It took all I had not to just kick him in the balls and leave him there at Walgreens while I took my girls far away from the drama and stress he constantly created for us. That is the honest to goodness truth. I went with paramedic lady's advice in the end. Paramedic lady seemed more like my style of woman. I piled all of us into the rental car, put the hospital name into my GPS, and drove over multiple Las Vegas freeways to get there. When it was his turn to be seen, I was not allowed into the treatment area with my children. Unwilling to leave my five and seven year old anywhere alone, I had no choice but to wait outside for hours with no idea what was going on.

As it turned out, the friendly doctor diagnosed my husband with bronchitis and gave him just what he needed to get through his withdrawal, which was five more prescriptions. He had forgotten to tell the good doctor about his little drug problem. Three of these new bottles contained medications with opioids. Perfect. That should satisfy him for a while, I thought as I drove everyone to the pharmacy.

The next morning, something strange happened. In the midst of the chaos, an old friend appeared by my side. It had been years since I'd felt her presence. Steely Resolve was her name. She was the one with the big girl panties. Never one to apologize for her entrances, Steely waltzed right in and said, "Hey girl, it's time to stand back up my dear."

Steely was as beautiful as ever, wise, finely honed, and unwavering. Always a source of inner strength and independence, that fateful morning she reappeared before me like a lightning bolt in the night sky. I didn't fully acknowledge Steely at first, more just a small wave and nod between us from a distance. It was like something you might find yourself doing with a once close confidante that you hadn't seen in forever. "Hello there old friend" I thought.

I was immediately filled with excitement, and then, dread. Because as exhilarating as Steely Resolve always was, I knew following her lead was inevitable. And this time it was at total odds with life as we all currently knew it, and my girls, oh, my girls. My heart was about to break into a million pieces for them.

That morning, I had insisted on taking them out for some fun after the stress of watching their father self- destruct. That is just when Steely arrived. As I stood in the entrance way of our hotel room, scattered with kids' shoes and toys, I went about my usual mom routine. "Get your shoes, grab some water, shhh...don't disturb Daddy because he is sick." I took one long look at Steely in the midst of the chaos, our eyes locked, and the decision was made.

As I ushered my girls out the door and listened to it slam shut behind us, I knew it was over. I hadn't only closed the door to the room; in that moment, I closed the door on my marriage. I didn't know how or when, but I knew Steely's call when I heard it. It was time to stand up and take back my life, our lives. My husband was in a downward spiral and if I didn't act soon, he would take us all down with him.

And with that, I took my daughters' little hands in mine and together the three of us walked down the hall and out of the resort toward the strip. Tough times were ahead, but right then in that moment we had a date to ride the Linq High Roller and live our best lives. After all, who wouldn't want to start the first day of the rest of their life riding the world's largest ferris wheel?

# 7

# WE ALL HAVE A SHADOW
VERONICA BOCCINFUSO

Often, we need to hit rock bottom to shed our old patterns and awaken to things we must address. For myself, this happened in 2019 when my husband, life partner of ten years, business partner, father of my children, and my rock told me he wasn't happy in our marriage and wanted out. They say that divorce is one of the hardest things a person can go through, next to public speaking. I would have to agree. I never saw it coming, but it was my rock bottom. When everything began to breakdown and decay, I was left raw and vulnerable. Looking back, as counterintuitive as it may sound, this actually made me ripe for opportunities and remarkable growth.

We all have seasons and phases in our lives that we must go through. I recall looking back on the winter of 2019/2020 as a phase of shedding layers. We are a part of nature, and just like the trees. Letting go and being stripped raw is part of the rebirth and growth process. When I was going through this storm of life, I was unable to eat, sleep, or think clearly. I would cry uncontrollably and couldn't help myself. I ached for my children as they witnessed their mother go through this pain and be unable to help them through theirs, as I wish I could have. I lost my appetite and my eye sight became blurry. I lost my ability to do basic math, and my hair was falling out. I felt as though I could barely function, and I would pace through the house over-thinking and replaying events over and over in my mind. My worries and thoughts controlled me. I often acted out of character and would then beat myself up over the things I said and did. I was emotionally dysregulated and so very far from feeling balanced. I was a hopeless wreck.

Like many women, I identified with the roles I filled: wife, mother, business owner, community member, daughter-in-law, auntie, sister-in-law, and friend. But I had now lost many of the roles that I previously and proudly saw myself through. My friend circle completely changed, and I wasn't able to show up as the same person that I had before. I was in a dark season. I no longer fit in with the stay at home moms and wives. Couples and networking events didn't suit me anymore either, as I no longer held these cherished titles. It was time to re-find myself. I reflected often on the questions "Who is Veronica really? What is my true identity, if it's not the Veronica that played my old roles?"

It was a season of stripping off these layers, habits, patterns, expectations, and routines. What does one do when faced with this gift of rebirth? Often, we turn inwards and seek coaching, counselling, and guidance while trying to listen to our own inner wisdom. Slowly, through this process, I began to find myself and worked towards building my life as a reflection of my highest self: the best version of me. I focused on where I wanted to go and who I wanted to be. I used "I am" statements, manifestations, visualizations, imagination, and play!

What does Veronica enjoy? Well, I will tell you: I enjoy feeling joy, love and peace. I let joy be my compass. It guides my decisions. What would make me happy? What would fill my cup? What does my body desire? Who nourishes my soul? I got back in touch with my being, the present. I studied the cosmos, the chakras, and dived into meditation and journaling. I sought wisdom from women that I was drawn to. The women in my community lifted me up, they carried me through this time. They were friends, doctors, fellow divorcees, strangers, coaches, yoga teachers, counsellors, neighbours, and community members. Women, it was the women who held me up during this time. And now I see, while men may come and go, sisterhood will always be there for me as a support and a foundation to my wellbeing. I read and read and read. I pushed myself out of my comfort zone as I learned to do things alone. I would attend events solo, seeking passion, and would leave with new friends. I discovered that everyone has a shadow if you take the time to pay attention. Even those 'high fliers' have shadows. We all have our junk, our demons, and our challenges. We are all human. This understanding has allowed me to be easier on myself. To feel emotion and pain is a part of the human experience. The trick is to be aware of it, acknowledging it, and then letting it pass rather than holding on.

Slowly, I began to find greater joy than ever before. I shed the stress that I carried for years when I was focused on achieving and checking off the boxes. I now focus on my mindset and strive for positive thoughts. Through my self care practice, I have become more in tune with my body, and can sense the moment I feel off, imbalanced, or have a chakra block. Rather than ignoring it like I once did, I dig in seeking to understand what is going on under the surface and address it. I want to live with clear channels, uncapped, and have energy flow. I wish to radiate love and joy, and have it be contagious for others.

I often experience throat chakra blockages, which means I am challenged to express my truth. Speaking authentically is my challenge these days. I keep working on it however, and sharing my story is one way to release this block. I hope to inspire someone to work through their pain and realize that there is light on the other side.

Now, just a year later, I have restored my health, become stronger, and am much more self-aware. I have manifested the community of women around me that I always desired. I have started a new company that resonates with my values and mission in life: to help others seek improved well-being through organizing, decorating, and creating home environments that bring them joy. This has been my dream career since high school, and I am finally pursuing my dream! It is never too late to pursue your own big hairy, scary dream.

As far as new accomplishments, I can now do a headstand and am working towards a handstand! My yoga practice has blossomed. My friendships have deepened. My ability to play and seek joy has grown. The greatest thing is that I now believe in my ability to attract into my life what I want. And ultimately, last year's major life changes may have indeed been what I subconsciously wanted all along. I attracted them to my life for a reason. I believe we attract everything into our lives, whether consciously or subconsciously. It is better to make conscious intentions than let our fears attract what we don't want into our lives. I always knew that one day my pain would be worth it, and I would be able to look back and have comfort knowing I was manifesting what was meant to be. I truly believe that everything happens for a reason. Everything needed to fall away in order to build me back up again and find myself. My hope is that my story will help to encourage others, going through their shadows, to turn inwards and answer the hard questions, leading them to take the necessary steps towards creating the lives they truly desire.

# 8

# ROOTS
HOLLY JONES

Did you ever wonder how you came to be, or what made you the type of person that you are today? Wow, now doesn't that sound deep!

I know it's a crazy question, but what if you were just not sure. What role did your genes play? After all, you can't control those. How about your upbringing from infanthood to child-hood, how did that part of life shape you? Or did you become who are you because of your life experiences through adolescence and into adulthood?

I will share my personal thoughts and reflect on the many blessings, yet hardships, that I have experienced and overcome in order to heal and reach answers. Not everyone's story or thoughts are similar to mine, and that is important for me to note.

Ever since I was a little girl my parents openly shared with me about the blessing of being adopted. They would let me know just how special I was, as I had been a "chosen" one from the orphanage. That always seemed to bring me happiness and comfort. Along with loving parents, I had one sister. She had been adopted from elsewhere in Canada, two years prior to my adoption. I remember a very simple life growing up. We did not have much in terms of material things, such as extra spending money, fancy clothes, televisions, toys, sports or treats. I remember that my dad worked very hard and to the best of his ability to provide for us while my dear, sweet mother had the difficult job of looking after our home. There were definitely times, as I got older and developed relationships with amazing friends at school, that I felt somewhat jealous and sad as I believed those material things I didn't have were important if I wanted to fit into the "norm."

My sister and I were brought up in a home filled with worship and religious values. Just to name a few examples, we were taught to obey and follow all rules, be kind and respectful, do unto others, complete daily chores, work hard, and prioritize our needs over our wants. As I grew older, I was expected to get a job at a very early age and help to provide for the family. In addition, I was to excel in school in order to ensure that I could advance with my education and choose a career. Unfortunately, the expectations placed upon my sister and I were different. Although we were brought up in the same environment, complete with love, structure and values, her chosen path included anger, resentment, manipulation and trouble. I often ask myself why I did not rebel and why I worked so hard at pleasing others and making my parents proud of who I was becoming? Was it because it was *expected* of me?

"You are not like your sister," they would say.

"We just know that you will do amazing things with your life. You are cut from a different cloth."

I reflect now on what that even meant.

"You will never disappoint us," they would say.

Was I born this way, or was how I acted learned behaviour? Perhaps I became who I did because I witnessed my sister's mental, verbal, and physical abuse for years. Could fear have led me to be who I was?

My mother adopted me when she was in her 40's and I idolized her. She was a very quiet, soft spoken woman. She didn't seem to have the zest for life and knowledge that I did, but she was just perfect in my eyes. She was so very special. Her kind simple gestures and sense of humor were such gifts. She was always chuckling to herself. Her batches of warm homemade cookies and her daily calls to just check in on me once I left home live on in my mind. Just her presence alone brought me such comfort- till death do us part. I kept telling her that she was going to live forever because I needed her. I miss her every single day.

In my 40's, I searched and was lucky enough to find my biological mother. She had actually wound up marrying my biological father years after my birth. As a little girl, growing up not knowing my biological parents, I often wondered and dreamed about my biological mother. I pretended that maybe I was a princess that lived in a mansion with dolls and toys and pretty dresses. This is probably similar to the things many little girls dream of. In my case however, I really could make up my own story of who I might truly be and where I may have come from. Believe me though, I never once felt anger, remorse, ill feelings or regret for the difficult choices that were made at the time of my birth. I look back over my years and feel very blessed and honoured to have had a birth mother who wanted me to have a chance at a better life than the one she could have provided at the time. For that, I will always be eternally grateful.

Through everything life has presented me with, I count myself a lucky one. I have loved life and have lived to the best of my ability with the resources I have. I've worked very hard, overcome many obstacles and learned difficult lessons. I've made both good and bad choices. Ever since I was a little girl, I had a desire to care for others. This is a huge part of who I am, and it allowed me to have a successful career as a nurse for 40 years. I cannot describe the fulfillment I experience through being able to care for my patients and their families, and to love, cry and laugh with them. My peers, co-workers, staff, students, and mentors have provided me with so much joy and led me to become a mentor myself. I have also been very blessed with an amazing husband of 40 years, and he loves me unconditionally. I have two amazing, driven children who make me proud every day. I also now have two precious granddaughters that bring me limitless, never ending joy.

Being a mother is one of the hugest parts of who I am. There simply are not enough perfect words to describe that gifted role. Nurturing and guiding my two little humans in a world with so much chaos and pressure led me to reflect daily while I watched them grow and turn into the loving and exceptional humans they are today.

So, how did I come to be? I believe that although I may have had good genes to begin with, my successful life is due to my upbringing and my values. Facing challenges at an early age built my coping skills and the ability to overcome. The support of my family was crucial, as were my experiences, studies, and life lessons, both good and bad. My friends, acquaintances, fellow peers and students, as well as patients and their families moulded me. We all have choices; I had choices. Growing up is hard. Life is hard; and change is hard. When I was down, I chose not to settle. I chose not to give up. The ability to love others unconditionally is a gift, and I've never looked for anything in return so then I'm never disappointed. I love to empower and be empowered.

A word of advice:

Be courageous. Believe in yourself. Be resilient, and just

know that the world is full of special people. We never stop learning, so be open to change and adapt.

Finding yourself may be easy for some but know that most things in life do not come easily. You must put in the work to manifest the results that you are looking for. The road was not always easy leading me to where I am today, but would I change it if I could? Absolutely not. I enjoy myself and who I have become. I feel honoured to have enjoyed friendships and amazing communities over the years. They nurtured me and set me on my path to success.

Here's to many more years of keeping my eyes wide open, and taking it all in just to see if I can find myself even further.

# 9

# MAKING UP MY MIND
ABISOLA OLAPEJU

Finding yourself is the starting point of creating your new identity.

Being stuck changed my life forever and gave me a new sense of myself.

I come from a middle class family. My dad worked in the bank as a quantity surveyor while my mother was a high school chemistry teacher and ran a pastry and nylon supply business as a side-hustle to make more money to support our family.

We lived a simple life with nothing fancy in addition to the basics. My father's work involved quite a lot of travel out of town while we lived in Lagos, Nigeria.

I spent most of my early childhood with my mom and siblings who eventually went off to boarding school.

Just like most young children, I had big dreams and aspirations. Born in Africa, I learned to embrace the richness of our diversity along with the unique challenges of our daily existence. I was exposed to the innovations of the developed world through the television. This expanded my imagination and birthed in me a desire to help solve some of our cultural problems. I had big dreams of making an indelible impact in healthcare. At that time, I was keen on finding the cure for HIV/AIDS and helping to educate the population about preventive measures and treatments that could improve life-expectancy. HIV/AIDS was the biggest cause of death in Africa and the disease was spreading rapidly.

My mum was a solid rock for me who encouraged my dreams and instilled strong values such as integrity, hard work and persistence. She was my anchor and my number one supporter. We shared a special bond.

My world crumbled at age nine when I received the news that my mother had died in a ghastly motor accident. It was less than 2 months away from my tenth birthday party which was being planned for me.

In the blink of an eye, the world I knew no longer existed. While arranging my clothes in preparation for a new phase of life, I found an audio recording of myself singing the lyrics to a song from Disney's Aladdin. I was caught in the moment of emotion, as I am a lover of music and nature. In an excited state, I climbed up on a stool to replay this recording on the cassette player, and I fell on the floor.

At first, I thought it was a mild injury which would eventually heal. Soon however, it started to swell and I until I could not move my arm. It turned out that a part of my bone was broken and I had to wear a cast for six months on my right arm.

My father had to go back to work and so my siblings and I moved into our grandparent's home. My grandparents are amazing people, and they did try to make us feel comfortable, but it was just not the same.

My heart ached for months and I did blame God for taking her away. I had quite a number of vivid dreams where I saw her again.

Before long, I moved to my uncle's house as I was quite in need of support and encouragement to even get dressed and take a bath. Truly, this was not the best of times. While moving through my grief, I experienced some wake up calls which sparked my sense of independence and resolute determination to go after my dreams and make my mother proud of me.

Being raised by a community has some perks. I was exposed early on to our diverse culture and learned to understand relationships. Through observation, I learned so many things such as reading and the importance of investing in my personal growth.

I passed my entrance exams at the top of my class and received admission into the same school that my elder sister attended.

Being in boarding school has its own challenges and perks. For me, it was another opportunity to keep learning and growing. I spent most of my teenage years here with only short holidays either spent at my Dad's home or with my grandparents.

All through school, I kept my grit and focused on the goal of scholarly success. The day came when I reached my first major decision bridge. I needed to select my career path between becoming a medical doctor or a pharmacist .

At this point, I knew I loved challenges. I knew I could handle tough, and I knew I had raised the bar. Ultimately, I knew I was made for more.

And yet still, this knowledge left me confused. My heart tugged towards becoming a pharmacist despite the challenges within the field, but my Dad preferred the medical doctor option.

For weeks, I struggled to make a decision. There were more points in favour of medicine than pharmacy. After careful consideration, I decided that becoming a pharmacist was my choice, and I would be very successful at it.

I was accepted into the pharmacy program at university, and remained quite independent with a keen focus on my goal until

I hit my second year and something changed. I took an elective course alongside other students from various departments. If you remember the song " Miss Independent" by Ne-Yo, it perfectly describes me. I became friends with members of my group, and they introduced me to a man who eventually became my companion.

In all honesty, it took me quite a while to agree to move the relationship forward, but eventually I had to admit that I had finally found someone to share my dreams with, and we clicked on so many levels just like Bey and Jay. I loved him totally and built my world around him unknowingly. I imagined our lives together right down to the fine details. At this point I didn't realize what an imagination I had.

Guess what? When the relationship fell apart, so did my life once again. I wondered how I could ever achieve my dreams? I had low self -esteem and constantly sabotaged myself. I decided to wait for him in hopes that we might somehow come back together, but my hope was misplaced. I was crumbling further into limiting beliefs and self-doubt. Even though I was surrounded by people, I felt alone in my world. Then one day, I woke up to a call from my best girlfriend. Her words encouraged me to become aware of just how urgently I needed to get my life back together. I had been in the same spot for two years. She gave me a book titled, *Spheres of Silence* which was the first time I was exposed to tapping the power within the mind. The journey of reinventing myself began here.

I immediately began conscious study of how to rewire the mind through various programs, books, and training including neuro-linguistic programming.

Reprogramming my mind initiated an inside-out makeover. I created and unleashed an unapologetic new identity and got my mojo back on fire!

I truly found myself and moved on to aligning with my

purpose. This led me to the creation of a company where I am teaching and helping other women move from being stuck into clarity of purpose and kick-ass confidence.

There is nothing as rewarding for me as the joy when my clients embrace their moment of truth and take charge of all that is possible for them. When I witness this type of growth, I am like a child who just got a lollipop.

# 10

# A TRANSFORMATION FROM WITHIN

TISH WALLIS

Looking in the mirror, I no longer recognized the woman staring back at me. The reflection that had once been a strong, independent, and goal driven person was now a woman who had lost her dreams, her self-esteem, and her passion for life. She was lost in a world where she did not fit in.

Although this reflection was now different, it was also vaguely familiar. Words such as shy, timid, insecure, quiet, low self-esteem and introverted were commonly used to describe me through my upbringing. Because of this, they felt normal. In my early 30's however, I discovered that none of those words described me at all. They were merely labels that had been placed on me from a very young age by teachers, friends and family members. What I didn't know then was that the mind is a very mysterious thing and when you hear something enough, you start to believe it.

Imagine a young girl dancing in the aisles of the stores as she shops with her mother, or sharing her life story with the strangers sitting behind her on a greyhound bus as she and her grandmother travel back to Calgary from Kelowna. This young girl is full of life, charisma and energy. Now imagine a slightly older girl always looking down and staring at the floor, hair draped in front of her face to make her feel invisible and blend in. She avoids eye contact, and has a voice so quiet that you have to strain to hear her. Both of these girls were me at various parts of my adolescence.

My path of personal development began when I was only sixteen years old. We moved around a lot when I was growing up and by the time I turned sixteen, I had already attended 8 different schools. Being the new kid every couple of years meant that you never really got to know people very well. Putting up that wall of labels meant that they wouldn't be able to get to know me either. I was an observer in my own life, holding myself back from my true potential and missing out on so many opportunities. Something inside of me knew that I had more to offer if only I could break through the negative self-talk I was thinking about myself not being outgoing enough, or being too quiet. Keeping in mind that this was over twenty years ago now and personal development was referred to as *self-help*. I'll admit I was too intimidated to walk down the *self-help* aisle of the book store for fear of being judged. I can clearly remember one particular day, approaching that aisle thinking, *People are going to think there is something wrong with me.*

Well guess what, people aren't thinking about you as much as you think they are. But I was only sixteen, and didn't know that yet.

As a result of my insecurities, my research was limited to the small selection of books in the school's resource centre. What I learned then, was that I needed to get out of my comfort zone and out of the box that I had placed myself in. I made a point to talk to someone new every day. My first job was selling lingerie, talk about embracing discomfort. I stopped using labels to define who I was as a person. I started taking ballroom dance lessons and even competed in front of an audience on several occasions. I'll be forever grateful to my dance instructor for helping me build confidence within. Yes, me, the girl who would sit at her desk disregarding the other student's presentations because I was consumed with what I was going to say. I would then stand up in front of everyone, hiding behind my paper while presenting. My hands would be shaking so much that no one could even hear me anyways. Once finished, I would sit back down and replay every detail in my mind, feeling nervous and embarrassed. All of these little steps that I was taking to build up my self-confidence and shine my light brighter were huge in my personal growth journey.

If you're wondering what happened, on paper it appeared as though I was taking all of the necessary steps to work on overcoming these obstacles. The thing is, I got really good at talking to strangers. People I would never see again didn't intimidate me as much because it didn't matter what they thought of me. Those closest to me however, I still couldn't open up to. I became a workaholic achieving the career goals I had set out for myself; but I was also hiding behind my goals and busy work life to ensure that I didn't have to expand my social network. I eventually got married and became a mom to two amazing boys who have taught me so much over the years. While being a mom however, I forgot to keep working on me. I stopped making time for myself, and I stopped doing the things I was passionate about. In turn, I quickly became that lost, insecure, dependent soul with no direction once again.

The difference was, this time I knew what I needed to do. I just needed a push. What I didn't realize at the time was that the push would come through an entrepreneurial venture that I agreed to almost four years ago. At that time, I had already been at home with my boys for four years, and was searching for an outlet: something for me, a project that would nourish my creativity. Because of this venture, my world became full of women and men with a passion for helping others succeed both personally and professionally. I had found a group of liked minded individuals with whom to develop friendships and build relationships. This was something that I had been lacking in my mom roll. Best of all, I was now a part of a monthly book club that was recommending all of the books I desired to read when I was younger. These *self- help* books have indeed helped me change my path, guiding me to become the person I am today.

Choosing this new path and surrounding myself with so many successful leaders has allowed me to find my voice. Having always had a passion for health and wellness, and having run my own mobile massage practice for 18 years and counting, I now had something new. I had fresh knowledge, encouragement, support, and a desire to share my passion for healthy living with others. Those who knew me as that shy timid girl still have a hard time believing the transformation I've experienced and how much I now have to share.

It has been an amazing journey so far and continues to be something I work on every day. My love for books, journaling, daily affirmations and self-care has helped me recognize, embrace and love the person staring back at me in the mirror.

# 11

# REAL LIFE PLOT TWIST
THERESA STADNYK

Who are you? Who are you really? I thought I knew who I was, and then I became a mom. As I sat there holding my first born and looking into his beautiful eyes staring back at me, I realized that there is so much more to life than what I understand. Having each one of my boys just solidified my love and determination to be an amazing mom. Life was no longer just about me! My last beautiful baby boy, number three, was born in March 2013. He completed our family.

As much as I loved having my boys, with each pregnancy, I gained a lot of weight. I needed to do something about it. I found home workouts, and slimmed down into the fittest I'd ever been in my life. I re-defined myself as a loving, committed, strong and fit mother. This accented the positive, outgoing and uplifting person that I already was. As a civil engineering technician, I design subdivisions, roadways, underground utilities, parking lots, etc. I've always loved what I do, but I wanted to spend as much time as I could with my kids. I accepted a job at SAIT Polytechnic in Calgary, instructing a night class on how to design civil engineering projects on the computer. I was loving life and thought I had found a good rhythm for myself and my family when life threw me an unexpected turn, and I got sick. Who I perceived myself to be changed yet again. What I have found, is that the answer to who I am is not an easy one at all, because it changes. In the words of my boys, like a Pokemon, it evolves.

In April, 2015 I got sick, really sick, while raking leaves in the backyard. And, because of a tick, my life changed.

A few months later I was teaching at SAIT and began leaking breast milk in front of my class. I hadn't breastfed a child for two years. The moment was significant and embarrassing. This actually happened a couple of times and was followed by horrible, dizzying headaches. On one occasion, I actually collapsed during class while I was writing on the white board in front of my students. I got back up and finished the class as best as I could, but the event triggered me to go and see my doctor. Because of my symptoms, my physician was worried that I might have a pituitary tumour, and I was put on prednisone right away while I waited for an MRI. In Alberta, I might wait for six to nine months to have this done. After starting the medicine, my symptoms started to worsen. My headaches started getting so intense that I became nauseous. My breasts were still leaking milk, and I was barely able to get myself into the classroom to teach. Then, the double vision began which made me very scared to drive.

My deterioration was affecting my home life. My husband was at work during the day, and I was struggling to get my two older boys to school in the morning and make it through the day with my two year old son at home. I knew something was wrong, but I kept focused on just surviving each day. Although I was scared to drive to work, I forced myself to finish the semester for my students, and I masked my head pain with pain killers. When I collapsed for the second time instructing my class, my husband took me to emergency. Unbelievably, a student reported that I was showing up to work drunk. I'm not a drinker.

I really didn't know how worried my husband was until I heard him tell the doctor that I wasn't able to care for my three young boys.

I was admitted to the neurology department, and they immediately ran a bunch of tests. My head hurt so badly that I had trouble focusing or carrying on a conversation; and for those who know me, I'm a talker. I can remember how bruised my arms became from so much blood work. Being rolled away to the MRI brought on a flood of emotions. Although I was nervous while being fitted for that helmet and while being told to stay completely still in the confining tube, I still did not think the worst. Not yet anyways. I remember that my head was hurting so badly, and all I could focus on was when I would see my boys again.

I remember being in a neurology ward hospital bed, with the lights off, and my husband by my bedside while hearing that every test had come back 'normal'. I could see the frustration on my husband's face with each test result. Since the MRI came back normal as well, they thought perhaps it was my spinal fluid. Maybe having too little of it was causing me pain. So, I had fluid collected from my spine for testing. What a painful test! I remember thinking that they must have taken too much fluid, because the pain was truly intense. Again, the test results came back normal.

I continued to go through every test imaginable. Each day it seemed like I had a new symptom. The worst of which was my eyesight! My double vision was progressively getting worse. It got to the point where I would need someone to read my emails and texts to me. Everything had to be done in slow motion too, or I felt like I was on a full speed roller coaster. By this point, I needed to use a walker to get myself to the bathroom. An ocular test was conducted with vision goggles that blacked everything out. Once they put the goggles on me, my eyes started darting around and they thought I was having a stroke. They called a code and I was rushed out of the room for a CT scan. Fortunately, it was not a stroke, and again the test came back 'normal'. As days went on, I developed a strange twitch. My joints started to feel like they were on fire. Nothing eased the pain. Then, randomly, and out of the blue, my arms and legs started to go numb. Infectious disease specialists were now involved and I was tested for so many conditions, including rheumatoid arthritis, lupus, strep, HIV and a plethora of others. I did not really understand what the doctors were saying, or what was happening. I was still just thinking about my boys and looking forward to the next time I would see them. I was now either bed ridden, or using a wheelchair to get around. Fortunately, I had a solid tribe behind me and someone with me most of the day, every day. I had many visitors including my friends, family, other moms from school, and neighbours. Everyone kept me smiling and focusing on positivity. I feel so very grateful and blessed that they cared enough to visit. I don't think any of them knew just how important their kindness was and how it helped me. I found out later that a bunch of my friends and neighbours were helping my husband by delivering meals to the house. It was so heartwarming and appreciated. Being there for someone in their time of need is the most precious gift you can give! Actually, now, if I have a depressed day, I choose to do something nice for someone else. It uplifts my mood immediately! Spread the kindness!

I am also so grateful for my husband. He was my rock. He was taking care of the home front, working full time, and with me as much as he could for close to three weeks. Upon discharge, my neurologist labelled me as having an 'A- typical headache'. I felt so sick and defeated that I just kept nodding and thinking, *okay, that sucks*. My husband did not take this as diagnosis. He remained by my side fighting for me because I was not well enough, nor in the right mind, to do it on my own. He got into a heated conversation with my neurologist and basically said that I could barely take care of myself, let alone my three young boys. It was NOT just a headache! I did not know this until later, but my husband was staying up late each night researching my symptoms. He brought up lyme disease with the neurologist after reading a blog about a lady experiencing similar symptoms to mine. Luckily, the neurologist had a colleague in the hospital that was the top lyme specialist in North America. He called him, I think in desperation, as my husband would not back down. The specialist was curious and wanted to chat with me.

We had a consultation, and he was certain that it was lyme. As he asked us questions, we recalled the bullseye rash on my back after raking leaves that April day. I get bug bites often, as well as marks and reactions to them, so I did not think anything of it at the time. But, we did not know about lyme disease. I had already been tested for lyme, but the test came back negative. I was encouraged to be tested again, and instructed on how to get my blood work sent to the University of New York. The results came back a few days later, and were positive for lyme, and a few nasty co-infections. Immediately, I started an IV antibiotic treatment. We were elated to finally know what was wrong. I cried joyful tears for a full day. Basically, my body was attacking itself and affecting me neurologically the most. I could not think straight, and my double vision and inability to walk properly were from my body attacking how my brain communicated with my eyes and legs.

I was so sick by this time, and had constant tics throughout the day. The pressure in my head created a fog that was so intense that I couldn't think straight. My joints felt like they were on fire, which left me screaming in pain. I could barely get to the bathroom on my own and was being pushed around in a wheel-

56

chair. I had a conversation with my husband about writing letters to each of my boys, just in case I wouldn't make it home to them. I truly thought I was dying. Unfortunately, I couldn't think straight enough to even dictate a letter for my young boys. It devastated me! I kept hoping that I had been a good enough mother that I would be remembered. I asked my husband to make sure that he taught the boys how to have fun and not be so serious all the time.

Luckily, once I started the anti-biotics, the improvements occurred rapidly. I was in for a long recovery, but hopeful once symptoms started to improve. I worked with a physiotherapist and learned to first use a walker, and then to use my legs on my own. It was a huge day when Matthew, my youngest boy, came for a visit and was able to hold my hand while I slowly staggered down the hallway of the hospital instead of having him see me use a walker, or push me in a wheelchair.

After a couple weeks I was sent home to continue my recovery and was put on a barrage of very strong medications. I tried to be very positive while in the hospital and had faith that I would be okay. Now that I was home, the reality started settling in. I needed so much help during the day and struggled to make myself something to eat. I wasn't able to help the kids, as it was hard enough to get myself to the bathroom. I was so grateful that both my Mom and my mother-in-law were able to stay with us and help out. We also had family, friends and neighbours pitching in as well. This was uplifting, and their kindness was a blessing that I will never forget.

It was like I was going through all of the stages of grief: denial, anger, bargaining, and depression. Although throughout my life I've always been upbeat, positive and uplifting, it was now difficult to hold onto my 'happy place'. I was angry and in tears all of the time, probably because I was so hard on myself. Five years later and I still can be. I remember thoughts such as:

I'm a horrible wife, a bad employee (could not work), and a bad friend. My confidence as a strong woman felt shattered. I did not recognize the woman in the mirror looking back at me. The worst part is that it's an invisible disease. A person couldn't physically see how badly I was hurting. I lost many friends as I had to keep cancelling plans. I had typically been the one calling, chatting, and initiating get togethers, but now I had to keep declining invitations as I was so sick from the strong medications, or simply could not muster the energy to make it through the day. The frustration with no one seeing my pain left me feeling so alone. When someone asked how I was doing, I reached a point of just responding with: I'm fine. But, I was most certainly not fine. I'm just not the type of person to complain or ask for help.

One day, a good friend told me about 'the spoon theory.' You begin by allocating yourself a certain number of spoons per week. Every time you commit to something, you take a spoon away. When the spoons are gone, you cannot commit to anything else. One spoon symbolized any task that used energy. Taking a shower could be worth one spoon; going to the grocery store might be worth four spoons; and going for a walk could be worth a whopping five spoons. This theory made me stop in my tracks. I was sad that I had to think about life on these terms, knowing that something simple such as taking a shower was using some of my valuable energy. But, this helped me in so many ways. It showed me that I needed to practice grace with my body. My amazing body was fighting for me and trying to recover and heal. I needed to be gentle with myself. No, I could not work out like I did before. Funny thing is, that is the one thing I missed the most and tended to dwell on. I was now gaining weight and emotionally eating because I felt sorry for myself. This was a bad combination. Because of this experience, I learned that working out is both a privilege and a gift.

Then finally, one day, I entered the final stage of grief: Acceptance. I was at one of my many doctor's appointments and was doing the cognitive test (done before each appointment). This is a test where you're asked to do simple tasks like draw a cube, clock, or remember words and repeat them. Believe it or not, on previous appointments, I could not complete some of these simple tasks. This had truly scared me. I was a smart gal! How could my brain be broken!? But, on this day, my specialist congratulated me for receiving 70% on the test. He was surprised because I was in tears after 'only' receiving 70%! Supportively, he reminded me of where I had been on our initial appointment. At that time I could not remember one word nor draw a clock! Yes, there were still things I was unable to do, but I had come so far. After all, I was walking and driving again. The elation I felt on the day I returned to work in an engineering office doing heavy civil engineering design again, was so intense that you could not wipe the smile off my face! I was finally proud of myself again. My confidence was slowly coming back!

Mindset is everything. I still have good and bad days, but I now choose to focus on the good ones, and what I *can* do versus what I *can't* do. I've also learned to be proud of where I am today and appreciate how hard I fought to get here! I've been in dark places in my mind where I feel hopeless and underwater. The scary part is that it's a slippery slope and you can and will stay there for a long time if you allow yourself to. I heard Dr. Phil once say, "You teach people how to treat you," and that speaks to how you treat yourself! Be kind to yourself. Allow yourself to have those bad days, but get up and shake it off! You ARE worth it, you ARE enough, and the world is better with you in it!

# 12

# UNAPOLOGETICALLY ME

AISHA AKRAM

The world isn't always as easy as it seems. On the surface, it seems like life is straightforward. We wake up in the morning, go about our daily life, go to sleep and repeat the day. However, it's now clear to see that life is an embodiment of thousands of tangled up emotions just waiting to be set free. From getting up in the morning, to getting back into bed at night, it's so easy to lose yourself. We spend so many of our days around other people that we often lose touch with ourselves and our own identity. In the past, my mind was like an unfinished puzzle and in some ways, it still is. I expended so much energy on finding the missing pieces, but it always seemed like they were so far out of my reach. The most difficult thing I've ever had to go through is losing myself because it is a grievance like none other. One cannot fathom how difficult it is to lose someone that's still living, especially when it is the person you're going to spend the rest of your life with: yourself. It felt as if I was carrying the weight of grief on my back. I was grieving the loss of my old self as if it were lost forever, without realizing that it wasn't.

It's understandable that when we enter adolescence we

struggle with identity. But I didn't realize what I was struggling with until I grew a bit older. It felt like I was stuck in this eternal state of uncertainty, not knowing who I really was or what I was meant to do. This was new territory to me, and confusing, because for others it seemed like I always had my life together and knew who I was. Pretending is so hard when everyone around you looks up to you and sees you as a positive and optimistic person.

Regardless, there were those that most certainly noticed that something was wrong. Although a few friends did try to help me, my closest friend, Anna, was the one person I confided in throughout this entire journey. She was present through every crying episode, every low moment, and every time she sensed something was wrong. My story would not be complete without mentioning how she helped me, and I'll be eternally grateful for everything she put aside to help me endure my darkest moments. It's so refreshing to have a friendship in which confiding is reciprocal and met without judgement.

When looking past all of the difficulties and the loss of my identity, it's clear that I went searching for answers in the wrong places and was seeking external validation. I looked to social media for inspiration about the 'beauty standard' during a time where diet pills, airbrushing, and photoshop were the biggest trends. Body dysmorphia is no joke. I spent years of my life fighting against my own reflection, and thinking that I was defective. I saw flaws in myself that nobody else around me could ever see. I look back at pictures of myself during the time where my body image was the most negative, and what I see now is very different from what I saw then. I was consumed by society's views and expectations of me, and didn't realize that the only person I needed validation from was the person in the mirror. It's so common to do things because we care about what other people think, but that's not a healthy way to live.

Thriving off of validation and crumbling under criticism are natural human responses. The thing is however, that it truly doesn't matter what other people say or deem socially acceptable. My turning point finally came when I acknowledged this, and realized that it didn't matter what anyone else thought. I could be whoever I wanted to be. I could be free to be myself, and give love and kindness to others. I could look the way I wanted to. I could choose to empower myself. It was all about me. For once, I didn't see it as selfish to put myself first because after a long period of being selfless and unhappy, I knew that what I needed was to focus on myself and my happiness.

Most people have this moment eventually. Some call it a lightbulb moment or a moment where something just clicks. For me, it came in October 2020 during the COVID pandemic. I was at my absolute lowest and had deleted social media for just under a week because I needed to focus on myself. I realized that I was at a point where I couldn't continue to live as I had been. I needed to focus on what I knew made me happy. I practiced some mindfulness, watched a few movies, and most importantly: I wrote some poetry. Poetry has always been a form of expression for me. I call it my personal therapy because the pages always listen and never make me feel like a burden. My social media detox allowed me to gather up my thoughts and put them out onto paper. This was a large accomplishment for me after a long mental block through which I couldn't write. I had tried repeatedly, but it seemed as though my ink was running dry.

'Still Have Me' by Demi Lovato played through my speakers and reminded me that I could be whoever I wanted to be, and even though I didn't have much, the fact that I had myself was the only thing that mattered. Realizing this was the first step towards finding myself once again. Music really can speak when words fail to touch the surface. My mindset turned around completely.

Although a time of misery, dread, and uncertainty, the pandemic allowed me the space to find myself again and consider what's truly important and what I'm meant to be and do. It helped me, through the gift of time, to clarify my purpose in life. I've always been passionate about mental health and empowerment, and I believe that sharing my personal story helps other people feel that they're not alone. My role-model is Demi Lovato because she tells her story in the most beautiful ways and was the first person I ever looked up to. In fact, she was the first celebrity that I knew of that opened herself up publicly to share her story and make sure others didn't feel alone through their struggles.

Collectively, all of this made me realize that my purpose is to have an impact. 'Impact' is a widely used word with many connotations. I want to share my story with the world and show everyone that if a young brown woman can rise again, then so can they. I want to tell the world what I wish I could tell my younger self: Give out love, but remember to give some to yourself too. Ask for help when you need it because seeking support is never a weakness. Always be kind to others because you do not know what somebody is going through. Take a moment to breathe when life gets chaotic because you deserve a break. Never feel obliged to stay in contact with someone that hurts you. Remember that even in the darkest moments, there is always a glimmer of hope within you. I want to make sure every young person out there knows that they are not alone in their struggles. I want to provide a stepping stone for people in order for them to get closer to finding their purpose. Abraham Maslow called it self-actualization, but it can be called whatever you want it to be. All of this is what 'impact' means to me.

Anyone can appreciate that changing old behaviours doesn't

happen overnight. Acknowledging that healing takes time is the first step. Healing is never a linear process. It's long and messy and sometimes feels like you've ripped off the bandage to reveal a wound that is endlessly bleeding. Although it still bleeds, this doesn't mean it can't be healed fully. I'm still in the healing process myself, but I've found my desired purpose which has brought me one step closer. It appears that every time I make an effort to align with my purpose, I'm one step closer to fully healing from everything that once ate me alive.

One important thing I've learnt from this whole experience is that the destination of this 'finding yourself' journey is inconclusive. We may find a purpose that ignites a fire in our bones for a time, yet still, continue to discover more every single day. There will be days where we progress further in this journey, and other days where we may not make any progress at all. But, for as long as our hearts continue to beat, we will need purpose. As we grow, we develop and unravel layers of ourselves that we never thought existed. We discover different versions of ourselves that co-exist. It's so beautiful to continue to bloom and discover more stunning petals growing: a symbol of the many layers of personality. Above all, as we age, we begin to accept the parts of ourselves that we used to find difficult to love. We learn to accept ourselves for who we are and not for who we are expected to be. It's difficult when expectations weigh heavily, such as in my community: the South Asian community. But happiness exceeds greed, pride and reputation any day. Family desire to maintain image should never overpower the need to be happy and content with life. Therefore, it's important to do what makes you happy, and doing this doesn't make you a selfish person at all. It just means that you have finally realized that sometimes you have to put yourself first.

Often, all it takes is a reminder that you are worthy of love and deserving of everything you give out to others. Finding yourself is one of the biggest challenges faced because identity crisis' are more common than some may think. They can tear you down to rock bottom, but once you fight your way out, you will begin to heal and fall in love with life again. Remember to be kind, be loud, be proud, and above all else, be unapologetically you.

# 13

## THE SPACE BETWEEN
KELSIE CHERNENKO

After having my son, I had a complete identity crisis.

I had heard that in the days, weeks and months that follow labour, mothers often experience an emotional rollercoaster. I was told to anticipate days of being emotionally wrecked and breaking into tears on the kitchen floor for no reason or simply out of love for my baby. I never experienced any of that. I was prepared, but the tears never came. What did come was much more frightening for me. First, it was numbness, followed by grief and anger, then eventually a spiritual awakening: a.k.a. mental breakdown.

My story is about the identity crisis that followed the birth of my son, and navigating the ugly emotions that surfaced in new motherhood. It's also about how I found my way back to myself. Although I was not officially diagnosed with postpartum depression, I certainly was not okay. I found myself in the space between suffering and adapting well to new motherhood.

The first eight months of motherhood were hell for me.

When people talk about having a baby, the narrative often centers around a deep, immediate, my-heart-is-so-full kind of love. They express how they couldn't imagine their lives before their baby. They now feel complete. By the time I gave birth to my son, I was going on day three of literally no sleep. I had suffered from insomnia throughout the last few months of pregnancy, which ramped up aggressively in the days leading up to labour. So, by the time Jackson was delivered, I felt as though I was floating outside my body, completely detached. I had thought that my lack of immediate connection to my son was due to my lack of sleep and the morphine, laughing gas, epidural cocktail. But, as the days turned into weeks, then into months, I still didn't feel that sparkly, obsessed with my baby feeling that every new mother was *supposed* to have. I *knew* I loved my son but, I felt nothing.

I also hadn't realized until my son was born that I was secretly hoping for a girl. I come from an entire generation of only girls, so the thought of having a boy was something I couldn't comprehend. The realization that I wanted my first baby to be a girl on top of my lack of immediate connection felt deeply shameful. I couldn't admit it at first, but deep down, I knew that the thought was there.

At the 3-week mark, as my body slowly began to heal, I confided in a few friends about my feelings of numbness. To my surprise, it was apparently a more common postpartum experience than I had realized. The more I shared my story, the better I felt and the more I learned that other moms had felt the same way. Once I was able to acknowledge my feelings, I was finally able to process and accept my reality. In fact, the more I talked about my feelings, the more I healed and felt connected to my son.

But that's not where my story ends. In fact, this was only the beginning.

In the first few months, I experienced severe sleep deprivation due to having to breastfeed every one and a half to three hours, as well as due to my son's inability to sleep (naps or nights) unless he was being held. Additionally, my own battle with insomnia didn't help either. We lived away from family, so our support was minimal. Then, the COVID-19 pandemic hit at five months postpartum, which meant no visitors or support, no mom groups or social interactions, no leaving the house for weeks, and fear of the unknown. Each day, week and month compounded, sinking me deeper and deeper into the hole of despair - I mean motherhood.

Although I had known that lack of sleep and a rough physical recovery were all part of what I signed up for, *living* and *experiencing* it was much harder than I could have imagined. Time lasted an eternity. The first eight weeks felt like eight years. By the seven-month mark, I *still* wasn't loving it and thought that something must be wrong with me. By month seven and a half, I had reached my breaking point and had what I like to call a "spiritual awakening" (a.k.a: mental breakdown).

In order for me to explain what led to my spiritual awakening, allow me to provide some context.

I'm someone who has been looking for 'my purpose' for my whole life. I've always felt as though I was *meant for something* but couldn't find what that *something* was, which left me with a certain emptiness inside. I tried to fill that void with distractions and general busy-ness.

My husband and I have always known that we wanted a family so we were thrilled that we were able to get pregnant. Although I didn't choose to have a child in order to fill the void inside me, I did think that once I had a baby, I would finally feel complete. But after my son was born, that empty space was still there and I felt so much shame. What sort of mother doesn't feel complete after having a child? Let me be clear, I love my son and my family more than anything, but that feeling that there was something more for me didn't go away. In fact, it magnified. I felt more lost than ever, like I didn't know who I was anymore.

Becoming a mom completely broke things open inside of me that I had been trying to suppress for years. It shattered into pieces who I used to be and now that the motherhood piece was added to my puzzle, I didn't fit back together again. I hit rock bottom in the identity department and it trickled into every aspect of my life, most notably my parenting and my marriage. Motherhood brought to the surface all of the sh*t that I had been running from for most of my life: a whirlpool of suppressed thoughts, feelings, anxieties, doubts and other emotions that had been there for a long time, but had been so tightly packed away under the clutter of my mental closet.

Then COVID happened, which meant no visitors, no leaving the house – no distractions. Add that to sleep deprivation compounded over seven months, next to no "me time," a baby that was a terrible napper and what do you get? A meltdown every few days as all of the built-up feelings that I had been avoiding boiled over. Without all of the distractions and busyness that I usually filled my life with, I was forced to feel all.of.it.

One of the emotions that came up frequently for me was anger, which surprised me because I am not usually an angry person. I felt anger and resentment towards my son when he wouldn't nap according to "normal standards" for his age. I felt anger towards my husband when he disagreed with me on a parenting approach. I felt anger when situations didn't work out like I expected them to, whether that be naptime, a trip to the beach, or an attempt to have a conversation with another adult. Ultimately, I felt anger whenever my reality did not match my expectations, and when it comes to motherhood, it rarely does. Motherhood has been so wildly different than I expected or was prepared for (despite reading all the books), that I craved to have some sort of control over it and when I couldn't control it, I got mad. I knew that I shouldn't express my anger towards my baby or my husband, so I quietly pushed the rage down until it built up to a point where it would unleash.

It is important to note that postpartum rage is very real. I encourage anyone feeling significant or long-lasting anger, or any symptoms of postpartum depression and anxiety that interfere with their relationships or ability to function, to seek professional help. Having said that, I challenge the notion that every uncomfortable feeling experienced by a new mom must be categorized as a mental illness. Anger is a natural human emotion so why must it get labelled as something clinical when new moms experience it? Can't we just be mad? The amount that we sacrifice in order to create and take care of a new human and the level of frustration that we deal with on a daily basis is substantial, so why can't we be allowed to just feel all the ugly emotions that come up without them being categorized and stigmatized? It is as though moms are not allowed to feel anything other than sheer happiness and gratitude for their little bundles of joy and if they do, that must mean that they are suffering from a postpartum disorder.

I think that as women, our relationship with "ugly" emotions stems from what we are taught at a young age. Many of us are raised to be "good girls" and taught that it is not ok to outwardly express feelings that are considered "masculine," like anger. As adults, this can lead to us suppressing and feeling ashamed when anger comes up, and not knowing how to process it. This does us a disservice because not only is anger a completely normal human emotion, it also contains valuable information about a need that is not being met or a boundary that is being crossed. So, if we can observe anger objectively, figure out what it is trying to tell us, and express it in a safe and healthy way, anger can actually be a very valuable tool in our growth as humans.

As difficult and painful as it was for me to feel the ugly

emotions, I knew that actually *feeling* them was a critical part of my healing process and that my "mental breakdown" was actually an opportunity for a Spiritual Awakening. I started journaling and counselling as a way of processing what I was going through and the "ah-ha" moments that came out of these experiences were staggering. For one, I realized that I wasn't as happy in my life as I knew I could be. I felt a lot of guilt about not being happy because my life is pretty great, according to society's standards. I also benefit from significant privilege given the colour of my skin and my upbringing.

So, one might wonder how I could still not be happy? I spent a lot of time reflecting on this through journaling and hiking in the forest with my 25lbs son strapped to me. The symbolism of his weight on my chest as I ascended the mountains and peeled back the layers of my soul was not lost on me. I discovered that my non-happiness was a result of me not feeling fulfilled in life and feeling like I had lost myself.

I think that one of the reasons an identity crisis can occur after having a baby is due to a deeply ingrained assumption that having a baby will make a woman feel whole. Statements like, "My heart is so full," or "I wasn't really living until I had children," and "I am now complete," are often associated with new motherhood. So when a new mother feels anything other than pure bliss and fulfillment, they feel like something is wrong with them.

I knew that in order to feel fulfilled, I first needed to rediscover myself. I decided to explore my soul, be accountable for my life and take action, which led me to finding personal development and coaching. Through coaching and counselling, I learned that no external person or thing will *ever* be able to fill the void within me. My personal fulfillment requires internal work that only I can do.

The first step for me in rediscovering my identity was to

bring to the surface, acknowledge and feel the thoughts and feelings with which I was struggling, namely that becoming a mom wasn't fulfilling me in the way that I thought it would (or should). Having a baby hadn't made me feel complete. It wasn't the solution to my feelings of inadequacy or the answer to the search for my purpose. Admitting these feelings brought me *so much* shame at first, but once I started to acknowledge them and just let them be, without judgement, they lost their power over me and I was able to release them.

I learned that it is okay to not love every stage of motherhood. It is okay to simultaneously grieve my old life and be grateful for my new family. It is okay to want to discover a part of me that has nothing to do with my child. And, most importantly, feeling all of the above doesn't make me selfish, a 'bad mom', or mean that I love my family any less. In fact, I believe it's the opposite: me discovering myself and setting a high standard for my own happiness sets an example for my family to not settle for a life of mediocrity. Contrary to the message we are given as moms, we don't have to sacrifice who we are - our needs, dreams and desires - for our family to be happy.

Once I let go of the guilt I had been harbouring around my experience with motherhood, and began to delve deeper into the personal development space, everything became clear and I realized that *this was it*. Not only was hiring a coach exactly what I needed, but it was also the answer to my life long search for my purpose. I knew, immediately, that this was my calling and that I would become a coach and help moms who feel unfulfilled by motherhood, much like I did.

Once I discovered coaching, I knew I had found an integral piece of my puzzle because I knew that being a mom is *part* of who I am but it isn't *only* who I am. Without the answer to the question: "who am I apart from being a mom?" I had felt lost and uninspired. Coaching, reignited the flame inside my soul, and now I'm blazing my trail forward unapologetically.

Although I didn't love the first year of motherhood, I am incredibly grateful for it. Having my son took me through one of the hardest periods in my life, but it was also the necessary catalyst for change. It took me hitting rock bottom in order to break, and only once we break ourselves open, do we create space for transformation. I learned how much mental and emotional grit, strength and resilience I have. I learned how to tap into my intuition, get comfortable with uncomfortable emotions, and advocate for my needs and boundaries. More excitingly, I found my purpose and the path to who I was meant to be.

**14**
---

# I AM ENOUGH
LINDSAY AMYOTTE

Have you ever been sitting in a room, thinking about how you just don't belong? That because you are a certain size, you don't deserve to be enjoying yourself, that you're not worthy of being there, that you aren't loveable, or worse than that, just not good enough? I have. Any time I would be out with my family, these ideas would permeate my brain, and ultimately interfere with my ability to be in the moment. This would happen even though being present and enjoying myself was something I really wanted.

I am certain that many women experience these thoughts daily. Why is this? We are all amazing beings; yet, something awful happens inside of our beautiful brains that tells us that this is not our truth. This was my reality a while ago, and was for a LONG time. It kills me to write these words and admit that I felt this way, or acknowledge that other women feel similarly. Sure, I still experience these thoughts sometimes, but they are fleeting now, and not my every day reality! What changed? Honestly, the answer is me. I changed.

January 1, 2020, I did what many people do, I set a new year's resolution to lose the large amount of weight I had been saying I would lose for the last decade. This was going to be my year, the year that it would all fall into place for me. Little did I know that a global pandemic would hit our world, and life as we knew it would be altered in inconceivable ways. My goal of losing weight was quickly halted when the world shut down and I, like so many others, was suddenly without a job and becoming a home-school teacher to my two children. My focus and drive for my goal quickly fell to the wayside.

Being at home for lengthy periods of time with nowhere to go and no one to visit, had me spending a lot of time thinking, or I guess you could say, wallowing. I wallowed in all I had lost, all I was missing, and all of the failures I had experienced, including the fact that I had not succeeded at my resolution. I had gotten to a really sad and hard place. I felt so defeated. Fear can take over all aspects of your life, including the fear that you are vali-dating your worst thoughts daily, and are unworthy of happi-ness. It wasn't good folks!

No BIG light bulb moment happened for me. I remain surprised by this because I always thought it would happen. I thought that if change was meant to be, I would have a eureka moment. Although it didn't happen that way, what did occur was just as life changing, but in a subtle way. Somewhere deep in my heart, I knew that sitting in my dark place wasn't what I wanted for myself or my sweet family. I knew that if I wanted to crawl away from this feeling of not being enough, I had to start deep inside and work my way out.

This realization began my self-growth journey, and led me to self-love. I wanted to be able to say, "I love me" with no when, and no because. Just the simple sentence "I love me" would be enough. I reached out to someone who I knew could help and started my journey. Ladies, it is okay to ask for help, and seek out a professional. We can't do life alone, nor should we have to. She allowed a place where I felt safe enough to be honest with both her and myself, and she challenged me to change the way I was thinking and slowly start to heal. In my humble opinion, every single person deserves somebody that they feel can help them do this work! And it was work... hard work. I was asked difficult questions, faced truths I didn't want to, and was pushed outside my comfort zone. But, little by little, inch by inch, I was progressing. I was slowly learning that the size of my body, what I looked like on the outside, or that DREADED number on the scale, did not need to hold power over me. I had always placed so many stipulations on my happiness. I had always thought that in order to love myself, I needed to be skinny. I believed that as if by magic, once I was skinny, then POOF: my self -limiting beliefs would disappear. Self- love would then take its rightful place. Wrong.

What I have come to slowly realize over this past year, is that losing the weight I want to lose will not ensure my happiness. I am the one with the power, not my scale, not my kids, and not my husband. ME! Like I said before, my world has not suddenly changed, and I am not running around with absolutely zero thoughts of doubt; but I have worked hard to be able to identify my triggers and negative thoughts in order to work them through and prevent them from taking me down a path from the past.

My hope for myself, as I continue on this journey, is to always know that I AM WORTHY, I AM ENOUGH and I AM LOVED. Period. No other words after, just I AM. And, I want other women to know this too, and to realize that no matter what, they are incredible and amazing people who deserve to live lives knowing that they have the power to choose, to choose themselves, and to choose love.

# 15

# PERCEPTION VS TRUTH

MELISSA PASUTTO

If finding myself means finding my authentic self, then I have arrived. I have known intrinsically and on a subconscious level, what the building blocks and pillars of my character have been since birth. The best part of knowing who you are, I have discovered, is that I have always liked the fabric of my character and my coat of many colors. I liked my set of beliefs and values and knew there was power behind them. The real problem was that others didn't. What I believed about myself and my life was not accepted and even considered threatening. So, my survival began, to change my actions, words, choices and habits. I survived to be liked, to be popular, to be included, and to present an acceptable me. I was just hoping and praying that someone would see me for whom I really was, not just the personified version.

Through my spiritual growth over the years, I came to realize that I also needed to take responsibility for how people perceive me starting with my outer appearance. I made an effort to change how I dressed so I would appear less intimidating. I wore fewer outfits with high heels, and toned down my jewelry and make-up. This failed.

Changing my conversation was next. I chatted less about my personal life, vacations I had taken, and fun with best friends. I eliminated discussions about dinner clubs that I belonged to, my husband, and my boys' competitions in snowboarding. Overall, I decreased conversation about me, and increased conversations about them. This failed too.

Perhaps then helping, assisting others, and giving advice would be more popular. Failed again. This attempt was received as me thinking that I knew more than they did, or that I was feeling sorry for them which caused them embarrassment. My good intentions backfired.

And so this is really where my story begins.

Finding myself has truly been a lifetime journey only because I thought I was lost, but wasn't. There have been many variables, events and challenges that were out of my control. These greatly influenced my trajectory, and included my upbringing, parental influence, living environment, birth order etc. All of these factors and more impacted the direction in which my life was destined to go.

Ultimately, I think it was the way that I was raised that gave me the best start to finding myself and manifesting the person I knew myself to be.

Let me explain. I was raised in a family of five, with a mother who longed for a girl through each pregnancy. But after the third boy, she was unable to have any more children. My parents decided to adopt a little girl, who ended up being sweet, loveable and a tomboy. Not someone for lace, ribbons, dresses and dolls. Why is this a necessary fact to share with you, you wonder? Wait for it. Four years after my sister was adopted, I was born. My mom did get pregnant after all, and lo and behold she had a little girl, that's me. "Landing softly," my mother would say. I was the girly girl she had dreamed of; bring on the lace and ribbons. From day one I was wanted, cherished, and loved.

The pink carpet was rolled out for me; not literally, but you get my point.

You see, I think finding yourself means being confident in your own skin, and liking and loving who you are. I believe this all began, for me, on the pink carpet.

My story continues with unconditional love, the key component to finding myself. As a child growing up, I received praise, encouragement and support from my mom. It's not that she thought I was perfect, but she would always word her advice in such a way that made me feel like I was already doing the right thing, or I had intended to do the right thing, but perhaps got distracted along the way. Her advice was communicated in such a way that made it sound like I was about to make the right choice, or I had already thought of a solution and maybe had just gotten a little sidetracked by other influences. Having parental trust as you grow up and develop, where your parents presume your intentions are good, is critical. I believe that the pillar stones and foundation of my womanhood landed softly on this safety net of unconditional love, which gave me the courage and bravado to find myself.

This unconditional love continued through my teen years and into my years as a young woman. This gave me confidence and solid self-esteem. Such confidence propelled me into adulthood believing that I could do whatever I set my mind to do. It gave me the drive to find my passion and vocation: teaching. This support, encouragement, and unconditional love instilled in me a sense of gratitude. That sense of gratitude only became greater as I became of service to the students in my classroom. Being of service created the feeling of gratitude. Gratitude led me to happiness. I enjoyed going to work each and every day, and being in the classroom to see the positive faces of the students. I loved my job because it was so rewarding to see students grow spiritually, academically and develop positive mental health habits. I was fortunate to have a job that I couldn't wait to get to the next day. My daily experience in the classroom gave me an authentic sense of happiness. I would, in my career, be the recipient of many accolades and awards which, not surprisingly, most often came from students and parents and not from my colleagues. To this day I have many more relationships with former students than I do with those I worked with. Children have an uncanny sense of seeing a person's character.

The unconditional love I received from my mother, as a child and adult, helped me maintain an optimistic attitude. I learned to relish in daily simple pleasures and look for joy in the gifts that each day presents. It sounds too good to be true, doesn't it? It's such a happy story so far.

Uncannily, some of the most painful experiences I encountered while finding myself, could actually have been linked to the unconditional love that I had received from my mom. That love gave me the self-esteem and confidence to propel me into a successful life, but not without heartache. Living in an environment where your parent believes and trusts in your decisions, and who you are as a person is an irreplaceable gift. However, it can also give you confidence that must not come off with arrogance, but with humility. This air of confidence can be interpreted, I've learned, as having a big ego. My persona was nonverbally communicating that I was perfect, a snob or too good for other people. This confidence was often perceived by others negatively. I didn't realize this until I was in high school, and conversing with a boy who looked at me and said, "You actually aren't the bitch, I thought you were!"

Being a confident person, I learned then, can be easily misconstrued as egotistical and intimidating.

To get back to where my story began, and how I found myself, I believe my up-bringing was key.

As a young girl my mother and I were always very close, and

we did everything together. We were best of friends right up through high school. As I mentioned, I really had my mother's understanding. She would actively listen to me, understand my intentions, and give me the benefit of the doubt. She believed in me and trusted in the depth of my character. This attitude and support she displayed gave me the confidence to make good choices and decisions in the future which included turning away from people in my life who had a negative perception of me. I remember walking through the front doors on the first day of high school, and saying to myself, "If I have to stand alone and be by myself, I will. If it means turning away from gossip and the mean actions of my peers, it will be worth it to be alone." And because I believed this, it was precisely what I did. I stood alone. My confidence was being perceived by my peers as me having an attitude that I was too good for them. I was excluded from many of my friend's activities, and not a part of any group. The consequences of my confident attitude left me without many friends. I basically went to school to go to class. Luckily, I had an equestrian life through which I could meet others and also a part-time job in retail that I enjoyed. Both of these distractions kept me occupied and connected to people who got to know me personally, and gave me a chance. At times, I was lonely. It was the first time I experienced judgement, and it hurt.

Unfortunately, judgement and misconstrued perceptions followed me right into my professional life. It saddens me now to recall some of the things that were said about me. All I really wanted in life was to be doing good for others. My intentions were pure, but my persona was misread and judged. People became jealous and exclusive. Although this was painful at times, I managed to rise above and remain steadfast in my belief of who I was, what I stood for and what my intentions truly were.

Finding myself meant living through the painful experiences

of perception and judgment.

Some people still, to this day, have a perception of me that a fairy godmother touched me with her magic wand and created a perfect life for me. Little do they know the crosses I had to bear and the hurdles I've jumped over in my life. I've experienced two sudden deaths in my immediate family: one being my father who died two days before Christmas, and the other was my brother, found dead in his apartment from an apparent massive heart attack. I've lived through a family bankruptcy, a brother with mental health issues, sibling divorces, being removed from a teaching position of twelve years that I loved, and a mother with cancer. These are just some of the examples of trauma that I've experienced in my life. The road wasn't always easy, and there's been no fairy godmother here.

Luckily, I had my faith and prayers to give me the strength and courage to be the best person that I could be. It was easier for people to put labels on me, such as: too intimidating, too eager, too enthusiastic, too dressed up, too... over giving me the benefit of the doubt or presuming goodwill.

Finding myself meant tolerating judgment, exclusion, and pain. Pain is not something that we want to experience, but it can actually be something that we grow from. My life looked perfect to the outside world because of the way I carried myself, spoke and my positive and happy attitude. All people saw was that I had a loving husband, two affectionate children, a fulfilling career, a beautiful home with nice things, yearly vacations to exciting places, and seemingly no monetary needs. It was the image of an ideal life. No one saw the effort or hard work it took to achieve some of these things. But everyone has struggles, including me.

What became critical for me through this survival process was mindset and how I would tackle the challenges that came on a daily basis. Attitude became more important than anything else. In finding my authentic self, I began to instill a mantra that reminded me that unless the person I was talking about was physically in the room, to defend themselves or speak on their own behalf, I should not be talking about them at all. This mantra came as a consequence of the judgement I experienced. Presuming goodwill and giving people the benefit of the doubt, accompanied with time to either explain or give further clarification, is also part of my mantra.

I have been the victim of pre-judgement by my peers many times in my life. So often I wasn't granted the opportunity to explain or clarify my thoughts or actions. I came to realize, over time, that this was basically due to jealousy and misunderstanding. Honest communication could have alleviated most of the misconceptions.

So, instead of becoming a victim and wallowing in self-pity, I stood tall, straightened my shoulders and went back to the core of believing in who I was. This did not include what others knew me to be, but only who I actually was. I was determined to continue fulfilling my passion and creating my best life. This meant continuing to love learning, to love my daily work, to spend quality time with my family and surround myself with people who would give me the benefit of the doubt. These were people who took the time to get to know me and trust me.

Since I made that conscious decision, I no longer worry about the judgement and perception of others. I have eliminated influencers in my life who judge me, or perceive me as superficial and intimidating. Instead, I surround myself with love and support from people I deem trustworthy.

I have always been a believer in knowledge and I gravitate towards self-help books. Knowledge empowers me. Empowerment encourages me to be the pilot of my own plane, and to get back into the driver's seat. In finding myself, I have accepted change. In fact, I embrace it. I take the detours knowing, from experience, that although they may not be planned, there might be something new for me to see or to learn about. There might be someone new to meet that I wouldn't have met if I hadn't taken a detour and embraced the change. I say, "yes" to change and 'thank you' to painful lessons. Had I of been closed-minded along my journey, and said "thy will be done," placing full faith in God to know what's best for me, I would not have experienced some of the happiest moments in my life. Those detours made all the difference. I now act on my conscience. I listen to my intuition, and my inner self. I am alert, aware, and I follow those instincts and callings. I experience joy through service and helping others, as well as from simple pleasures. I embrace what I can do for other people, and practice simple acts of kindness every day. I've come full circle back to whom I was at birth. My authentic self: realized.

I am, however, still trying to find my voice.

Finding my voice is an ongoing project. I first needed to find my voice in my marriage. And, after thirty- five years of being together, I'm glad I did. Several years of relationship coaching assisted me with this. It takes continuous effort on my part, and it does not come without heartache, worry and some discouraging times. But, that's ok. Life is about order, disorder and then reorder. So, I know it's natural. I just keep pushing through, not giving up, and working to achieve what I want to see manifested in my relationship with my husband, my sons and extended family.

Over the years, with the help of self-development books and coaching, I have been able to arrive at a place where I feel determined to stand my ground. I feel like I know what's best for me, and what's right for Melissa. This voice is not always well received, which can be discouraging and a temporary set-back. When this happens, I reset by getting quiet, and regrouping internally. Having my voice overpowered can sometimes make me want to soften my voice or lose it all together. This has happened to me periodically throughout the years; but, the older I get, the more determined I become. As the cliché goes, if I had known then what I know now, I would have had a stronger back bone.

So, what is keeping me from reaching my full potential? As I am still continuing to find my voice, it is pushing through and over the hurdle of confrontation. I hate conflict. So, you are probably saying to yourself, well why can't you just do what you want to do? Sometimes it's just not that easy. Your decisions, ideas, and actions can impact other people and knock them out of their predictable routines, presenting some unwelcome changes into their lives. This might create fear for them, and result in reactivity. The end result could be conflict unless you have winning strategies in your toolbox.

I do believe that if you do what you want to do and find your voice, you will be truly happy and content. No huge home, vacation properties, or beautiful gifts can give you the satisfaction you desire. Finding your voice will benefit your partner as well. When your partner is happy for you, you'll be happier together. That's truthfully a little easier said than done, but I keep working on this challenge.

Every day, I start fresh with a positive, and happy attitude. I'm ready to embrace whatever the day brings. My mom use to say "If you wake up, say thanks be to God and then get the day started." I believe that my tribulations, involving unfair perceptions and judgements by others, have made me determined to refrain from judging others, and to instead give them the benefit of the doubt. This is especially important in a time when people are so busy, and rarely have time for an actual conversation. Conversations are where we can gain knowledge, and clarify why someone did what they did or said what they said.

Arriving now in my time of retirement, I chuckle at the fact that I still may be trying to find my voice. Now, instead of arguing or needing to be right, I find solace simply knowing what's right for me. I don't necessarily always need to voice it, and eventually people around me will realize that they were wrong and perhaps I was right. I have come to accept that I will probably be mis-judged throughout the rest of my life, but it is really out of my control. I can only surround myself with people who want to get to know me, trust me, and actually like the person that I am. People who direct negative energy towards me, remind me of standing in front of a vacuum: they suck the positive energy right out of me.

Finding my voice is a continuing project for me, but I have been blessed in so many ways. I take the time to celebrate small daily blessings. When I say that I am still trying to find my voice, it means that I stay hopeful, and continue to be enthusiastic. I continue to want to learn more, read more and say yes to opportunities that arise. I do not take life for granted. I continue to write, and do personal development work; but, what I need to do more of, is to act on opportunities that ignite my passion. I need to put clearer intentions out into the universe, take action, and communicate my truth to others. I need to listen to my inner voice that tells me to play, have more fun, and share my story. This is not to be lazy, but to push myself on a daily basis. If I do these things, I will find my voice.

I'm not sure if I needed to go through the pain of judgement and misperception in my life to arrive at where I am today. And I most certainly would not wish some of those experiences on my worst enemy. But, I am where I am; and I'm looking forward to using my voice in a positive, inspiring and motivational way in the future. I have found myself, but I was never lost. In order to honour the unconditional love and support I received as a gift from my mother at birth, I now need to find my voice and use it to educate, support and love others.

# 16

# IN THE DARKNESS

JOY LAUGHREN

I sit, letting the silent darkness envelope me like a thick warm blanket. I rest my head back into the rocking chair closing my eyes and sinking deeply into the comfort of the chair. A tiny hand holds tightly to my long hair as a warm soft head rests in the nook of my arm. An almost inaudible breath escapes her and warms me physically and emotionally. Here, in the darkness of this room, everything is warm. In this room I feel love and peace but most of all, I feel unconditional safety. In the darkness I have permission to feel.

I'm sitting with an infant baby in perfect stillness, and in this quietness, this is who I let see me. She doesn't judge me or look at me differently when I show myself to her. She knows everything about me, and yet loves me with the kind of love I have been seeking my whole life. I sit here day after day, soaking in the safety, feeling the peace, and embracing the love. I am thankful that I cannot avoid the darkness.

I hear my thoughts and realize that they are tamed. In the warm safety of the darkness I have to listen; in the darkness I have to be quiet. I hear myself wish for my tiny baby to dream big, and instantly realize I have snuffed out all my own dreams. I listen to my mind wander through excuses but, in the darkness, I decipher that I am trying to deceive myself. It is not safe to be tame in the darkness.

I push my hair out of her hand with a smooth motion replacing it with my thumb. She relaxes and accepts my hand and then tightens her grip. I smile. In the darkness, her love and attachment erase pain and tension from inside my body. I hold firmly onto her perfect hand, most of her arm fitting inside my palm. The acceptance flowing from her body to mine relaxes my shoulders like a drug. A deep breath fills my lungs and complete love fills my soul. In the darkness I find true rest.

I see flashbacks of myself repeatedly apologizing for things that make me who I am. A silent tear escapes me as I regret hiding myself. In the silence I imagine my tiny baby unapologetically herself as she turns 25. I see regret for disowning things I love as if looking in a mirror. Regret for hiding myself and apologizing. In the darkness I see things clearer.

A night light glows a warm golden hue in a small corner of the darkness. It lights up only what is closest and leaves the rest of the room in its darkness. The light teases me, I long to be in the light. To be visible to others, I am tired of hiding. I ask myself, "Why can't I be in the light?" "Why am I hiding?" "Why don't I rest?" ...why? ...why? ...why?

In the darkness I feel past rejections evacuate my body embodied in tears running silent down my cheeks. I pray to God, and every higher power, that I can give my tiny babe what she needs to not know rejection. If you get enough acceptance, love and connection will you need the darkness? When every tear is gone I wonder, if I had felt no rejection what would life feel like? If you never feel sadness can you still feel joy? Do you still need the darkness?

The grip on the tiny hand has dissolved. The breath that warmed me physically and emotionally has deepened and almost vanished. The tiny babe is sound asleep. I am not ready to leave the darkness. Safe, warm, and full of love I sit a little while longer. Thinking my thoughts. Feeling my feelings. I know I will be back tomorrow, that I cannot avoid the darkness; but I am not ready to leave.

Darkness is not forever, you cannot control the darkness. I could not avoid the darkness, it was an inevitable end to each day. Inevitable quiet time where my body stopped to think deeply, control less, feel more, and just rest.

For me, it ended faster than I would have liked. That tiny baby grew into a toddler, and then a child. Now, we rarely sit in the darkness together, but when we do get a moment to sit quietly together I relish in the comfort of that dark, safe blanket and think of all the things a tiny baby taught me with her quiet acceptance.

The less I apologize for enjoying the things I love, the happier I am.

The less I hide the things that make me who I am, the happier I am.

The less I shush the voice of my conscience, the happier I am.

The more I wear the sassy one shoulder sweater, the happier I am.

The more latte oreos I quietly eat in the dark pantry, the happier I am.

The more I share the things I love with the world, the happier I am.

The more I embrace myself with radical self love, the happier I am.

Sometimes I imagine that baby one day, fully grown and also a mother. Sitting in the same chair holding her own baby, as I watch her from the doorway with adoration, love and respect for my best teacher.

# 17

# SURRENDER
ELANA VAN DEVENTER

I laid myself down on the bedroom carpet yet again. It felt like I was lying in front of a train, helplessly counting down the inevitable minutes until the crash would destroy everything. My marriage was already a disaster - dreaming of divorce, yelling through gritted teeth so the kids hopefully would not hear us.

I had wanted freedom and ended up more confused than ever. That bedroom carpet was becoming my only safe place to accept defeat. I had to perform everywhere else.

That afternoon, I waited for the light of the train to catch my eye. I waited for everything to be broken into pieces. I raised my hands over my head in total surrender with tears in my eyes, anticipating that either I would have a mental breakdown and become numb to my pain or I'd be so broken into tiny pieces, I'd never get myself together again.

Honestly, I'd tried everything I could think of to stay together, and that had nothing to do with my husband. How could I even bother to mend a tattered marriage when I was in shambles all on my own? This had been years in the making, and breaking.

Unfortunately, I'd never gone to university as I'd secretly

hoped to so many years before. Reluctantly, when I was pregnant with our first child, I quit my career in accounting, which was the first place I'd been perceived as smart. Then, the endless days of diaper changes and spoon-feeding toddlers just echoed a lie I already believed.

*You're not good for much.*

When our family of four moved across the ocean to provide better opportunities and quality of living for our children, as well as to give my husband a chance at a new intellectual challenge, it was as if there was no room for me to pack my dreams, too.

Resentment boiled into hot rage within weeks, as we pioneered the frigid belly of our first Canadian winter in a small town like the one I grew up in. The familiarity plunged me into a deep unrest in my soul. I was right back where I started.

They had been wasted years. Everything was ashes. Haunting me now was my childhood memory of the little girl who was afraid to speak in front of her class because she couldn't read without stammering. Now, I was in a new culture with a new language and an accent that made me stick out. Every bodily sacrifice of sweat and surgery in order to land a modeling contract (proof that I was good at something) was laughable as I donned a puffy winter coat and clunky snow boots. The inner circle of prestigious opportunities? Where were they now? The closest thing to fashion were the magazines in the grocery store.

It was pitiful how I had believed I could disappear from my past without healing it first.

The light that caught my eye that afternoon wasn't coming to roll over me. It was coming to meet me, the real me. In a moment I can only describe as Heaven, truth was illuminated inside of me. The 3-year-old girl who suffered a brain injury and was told she'd never be smart didn't have to believe that lie. The young woman who was told she was only useful for being quiet and looking pretty, didn't have to believe that lie. I didn't have to believe anything about myself except what was eternally true.

I was valuable.

I was loved.

I was made for a purpose and full of potential.

That was it. That was unchangeable.

In a matter of surrendered seconds, the worst and lowest moment in my life occurred. I thought I was going to lose everything, and I kind of did. I lost everything that wasn't raw and purely me. After 38 years of layering on anything that I could hide myself in, it had all become too heavy for me to bear. Being emotionally and spiritually exposed in that love light was the most radically unashamed act I could do for myself.

I wept in triumph for my newly found freedom, and for finally being able to come home to myself. It was a glorious end to the mental and physical punishment I had inflicted on myself so regularly.

That stunning light of palpable transformation suddenly called me deeper yet. If I had been trapped for so long, maybe I wasn't the only one. Maybe my surrender could become someone else's survival guide. I decided right there before getting up from the carpet that I would dedicate my life to fighting for the freedom of women and girls all over the world who were trapped just as I had been.

It's funny how I fought so hard to catch up with my purpose when all I had to do was give up and it would come rushing in. All on its own.

# 18

## CHOOSING HAPPINESS

ALLISON SILVAGGIO

I thought it would be fitting to make a cup of tea and begin writing today of all days. Firstly, it's January 5th (my eldest son's 15th birthday). How does this happen?

And, today I received my 200 Hour Yoga Instructor Certificate in the mail. I am extremely excited about this accomplishment and cannot wait to get started.

I believe that throughout a person's life, they can experience more than just one 'ah-ha' moment. I think I have!

2020 has been a trying year that has pushed most people to emotional levels that we have never experienced before. My first profession (other than recently adding yoga teacher), is travel consultant. It has been 23 years in the travel industry, and I feel like I could write a book on everything that has happened. There have been tremendous highs and lows, memorable experiences, and amazing people that I have met. I would not change a thing...well, maybe just one!

Have you ever travelled to a different country, a different continent, a different time zone and felt right at home? This first happened to me in Iceland about ten years ago. After departing the plane and taking a breath of what might just be the cleanest air in the world, we toured Reykjavik and the south coast for five days. The majority of our time was spent out in nature on excursions such as horse-back riding, glacier walks and boating tours. The entire time that I was in Iceland, I felt peaceful and free. I could breathe effortlessly and see things in a different light.

To continue with my journey in travel, boats are normally not my favourite mode of transportation. That being said, when the waters are calm with the sun on your face and birds flying overhead, I could truly become a sailor. I have been extremely lucky to experience not just one, but two expedition cruises. My first fantastic experience was north to the Arctic in 2012 on the Northwest Passage, which began in West Greenland and we sailed through to the Canadian Arctic. The second journey was in 2017 to my seventh continent, Antarctica. One of my favourite travel memories was sitting on Cuverville Island with what felt like over 2000 penguins walking around and sliding in the snow. I cannot tell you for how long I just sat and took this all in, putting the camera away and enjoying only the sounds of crackling ice and penguins. During meditation, I sometimes picture myself back there to help clear the mind and breathe.

Next, onto Motherhood. I have been blessed with my two sons: Nicholas, now 15, and Liam, 12. I truly believe that my main purpose in life was to be a mom! It was not easy in the beginning as I suffered from postpartum depression after having both children. However, with the help of both therapy, friends and family, it did not last long, and motherhood has been the most amazing journey. For anyone that suffers from postpartum depression, I highly recommend reading "Down Came the Rain: My Journey Through Postpartum Depression" by Brooke Shields. While reading her words, I realized that I am not the only one going through this, and it is not my fault. I believe that once you can stop blaming yourself, you can begin to heal and move forward.

After all these years, I still feel so blessed and fortunate to have these boys in my life and sometimes wish that I could freeze time to make it last longer.

And, finally to completing the 200 hour yoga instructor class. This was truly a life changing experience for me, and 2020 may have been the best year to learn more about breath and meditation. It is amazing how easy it becomes to study when you are absolutely invested in what you are reading and learning. I had already been practicing yoga for quite a long time when I decided to further my knowledge; therefore, I was fully aware that yoga is so much more than just stretching. The amazing part is how the practice can affect your life both on and off the mat. I am now able to take what I have learned and apply it throughout my day, in relationships with other people, and with meditation for a better sleep.

It sometimes feels like you are having the worst day ever, and nothing is going your way. So, you stop, breathe and notice the beauty in something so simple, such as the morning frost on a tree. It is truly amazing what you can train the mind to do. I once heard a saying 'finding happiness or choosing happiness.' Society is waiting for something to happen so we can be happy, but we forget that we are in charge of our own happiness. If going for a walk every day makes you happy, then do it! We all have the power to be happy, instead of happiness being something that we are waiting on or looking for.

In summary, I have had several moments throughout my life that have helped mould me into the person that I am. I can remember a few years back, having little self-confidence and constantly doubting the decisions that I made. Still a work in progress, I feel more content and complete than ever before. It is amazing how powerful memories are in your life, and how we cherish them. Now it is time to go and make some more!

# 19

# YOU JUST KNOW

LISA WEBB

I was 27 the first time I interviewed to be an assistant principal. My Master's in Educational Leadership was complete, and the prerequisite courses in educational administration were done. I was ready for the job.

"We appreciate your ambition, and you interviewed very well, but we feel like you need a bit more experience."

I was devastated. I wanted that job. In the interview debrief I asked them what I could do to be a successful candidate in the future. Instead of pouting that I didn't get it, I spent the next year making sure I did everything they said to do. I wasn't too proud to look at my blind spots. The next year when the job postings came up, I polished up my resume and gave it another shot. They were impressed by my tenacity. Young for the job or not, I became an assistant principal in my 20's and I was so damn proud of my hard work. I knew this was only the beginning of my career in education, and I had big dreams of where it was going.

Before long I met my husband, and quickly after that he was transferred due to his job. Together, we moved overseas and I spent the better part of a decade moving around, recreating my life, and trying to find my place in the world.

In those early days, I cried all of the tears there were to cry as I mourned leaving my promising career.

I gave birth to two children abroad, and they became my whole world, but I still needed more. I needed something for me. As much as I loved my children, motherhood wasn't the only thing that defined me. That girl with the ambition was still living inside of me, and after a few years of ignoring her, she started poking me from the inside as if she was saying, "Hey Lisa, remember me?"

After enough self-nudging, I decided that I needed a creative outlet. I didn't even know what that was though. I became a runner. I was running half marathon distances on the weekend, but it wasn't a job. Running gave me something to do with my time, but it wasn't fulfilling my longing for a purpose.

One wine infused night with some girlfriends, while living in France, the idea arose that I should start a blog. It wasn't a *real* job, because I didn't get paid, and at that point, I wasn't even a writer. But it scratched my creative itch and I just started from where I was. Turned out, I could write. I became tenacious about it. Thoughts, feelings, emotions and passion, they were all put into writing. I wrote my way onto some big websites, and became a regular contributor of The Huffington Post. The blog turned into travel writing, and the travel writing turned into books. I was a keyboard warrior who never saw it coming. This was my new career of choice.

Writing, as my passion project, worked out well until we needed a break from living abroad and moved, yet again. It felt like forever since we had lived at home. We left as newlyweds, and now had grade school kids who didn't have the slightest clue what it meant to be Canadian. We needed a stop at home.

My husband requested a transfer but the economy in Alberta, Canada wasn't exactly booming at the time.

"I'll take my severance and then just figure it out." He told me.

I panicked. One of us needed a job! Sure, I loved writing but it wasn't exactly bringing in the salary that our family needed to pay the bills.

"Someone has to work," I boldly stated as I opened up my laptop and instantly started researching how to reapply to the school board I once worked for.

I threw myself into the process, as I always do, and before I knew it, my online interview was complete and I had a signed contract and school assignment for the upcoming year. I was going back as a teacher, but knew I could work my way back up.

The universe uses funny timing when she wants to. Once my contract was signed, a position was found for my husband in Canada. My panic to get working was a bit premature, and not completely necessary. For the first time as a family, our kids would have two parents working full-time. We weren't sure what this would look or feel like.

Turns out it looked messy and felt awful. Our rhythm of life shifted abruptly when we moved to Canada and I learned for the first time what the term 'rat race' meant.

We went from being slightly spoiled overseas, to running around between jobs, groceries, school pick up, and activities. When did people have time to socialize? I never had a chance to go out anymore.

I decided to take matters into my own hands and try to recreate the vibe of the women's associations that had become my lifeline while we were overseas. They would plan events where you never needed a formal invitation, and everyone was welcome. It was a great way to meet people, and it gave me an excuse to take off my leggings, get properly dressed, and leave the house at least once a month. A guaranteed night out, that's what I needed in Canada.

"I think I'm going to try and start something," I said to my husband over dinner one night.

"Start something?" He raised an eyebrow. "I feel like we just landed in the eye of a tornado. We can barely keep up with our laundry, what could you possibly need to start?"

I told him how I missed girls' nights and meeting new and interesting women. I had come to thrive off of the energy in a room full of women. I wanted to build that.

At work, I was told that I had to put in my two years of probationary teaching again before I could reapply to administration. At the time it felt like a loss, because there was a leader in me just craving to be let out. But, I've come to see that disappointment as a gift.

Since I couldn't focus on administration, I'd spend my time teaching, and navigate this passion project in the cracks of my day: before my kids woke up, at recess, lunch, after school, and after my kids went to bed. Suddenly, my fire was back; and I was trudging forward with full force, building an idea that would create a community of, and for, women.

I learned, from building my writing career, that there would be failures along with successes; but I'd focus on riding the high of the wins, and using that momentum and energy, without being too hard on myself.

Putting my idea out into the world was a scary thing. What if no one showed up? What if it was a flop? Looking back, I can't actually believe the amount of bravery and courage it took. My secret sauce? Don't overthink things. I had an idea and went for it without sitting around too long wondering if it would work. Because, if I did that, eventually I probably could have convinced myself that it wouldn't.

Working at both teaching and getting my idea out into the

world was hard, but not impossible. After I held the first Wine, Women & Well-Being event, and experienced the energy in the room, I was hooked. I knew that this was something that could be a *thing*. If it worked here, in Calgary, it could work anywhere. I'm not the only one who craves community, connection and belonging. We all do! But there comes a time in our lives where it can be hard to know where to find it. My time overseas taught me that it's a common thread between all women, everywhere in the world. That's where the magic lies. We all are better versions of ourselves when we're surrounded, supported and uplifted by other women. Once I realized this, and recognized that I had the power to create that for other women, there was no turning back. I had found my calling. I had found myself. Being in a room surrounded by inspiring, empowering women is where I am my very best self.

We grow and change as we move through the seasons of our lives. I don't yet know if this is simply a chapter of my life, or if this *is* the story. But, just like when I found my husband, and found myself, the only way it can be described is, 'you just know.' I'm right where I need to be. It's a magical cocktail of doing what I love, being good at it, serving others, and spreading joy. It took me 40 years to get here, but boy does it feel good.

# 20

# THE MIRROR HAS TWO FACES

MARTINA PINTO

She looked up at the blue skies with cotton clouds that passed over her head as she cheerfully hopped around wearing her new birthday dress. She would be six years old, as she cut the birthday cake that day. Angela was extremely humble, kind and compassionate with a smile like sunshine. Like every child she loved gifts and especially the ones wrapped with glittery paper, where the light bounced off on her face.

Guests invited for the party began to arrive at her residence and Angela's happiness knew no bounds. Among the guests was her Aunt Fella, who presented her with a gift and insisted she open it in front of her. Even through Angela was instructed that gifts needed to be opened only after the party, she felt that it would displease her Aunt, so she unwrapped the gift. Suddenly there bounced the reflection of sunlight onto her face, as she tried to keep her eyes open.

It was a glass mirror attached to a wooden frame with floral designs carved into it. She looked at the reflection of herself and smiled. Aunt Fella was standing right beside her. She bent down and whispered in Angela's ear, "This is a magical mirror, it never lies. It will show you your flaws so that you can change them." Angela was delighted and considered the gift to be precious.

Days flew by and one afternoon, while returning from school, Angela's classmate Ruth commented on her hair. She said, "Your hair is just too curly and unlike mine that is so straight. You might be finding it very difficult to comb." While Angela didn't like what her friend had said, she thought of her mirror at home that never lied. Straight away, after returning home, Angela went straight to her room and looked into the mirror to view her curly hair. She immediately felt like the mirror was indicating a flaw. While there was nothing that she could do about it, she always carried the idea in her mind that she had to change the way her hair looked.

Angela was a quiet child by nature, and often heard her relatives say that she was shy and timid. Each time Angela heard something said about her, she ran to the mirror to confirm its truth. To her despair, the mirror would always said yes.

As Angela grew up, she began to find great joy in helping and comforting others. While some were grateful for the help, there were a few who moved away from her. Some drifted peacefully, while others told her that she was the reason they had to move away. Each person pointed out her shortcomings and limitations.

Each time a flaw was pointed out, she would reconfirm it with the mirror that always said yes. She now carried her imperfections, like a burden, to every gathering, conversation and to her pillow at night.

One day, Angela had a huge quarrel with her best friend. It broke her completely. To fill the void, she began taking morning walks. After a few rounds, she would sit on the bench and look aimlessly into space. Observing her daily routine, an old man walked up to her and asked "What troubles you, my child?"

Angela gave the old man a cold stare and looked away. The

man continued speaking, "Enjoy the journey, you are so young and have so many things to do." Hearing how blissfully he spoke about life made her fume from within. In that rage she looked at the old man and said "You don't know how it feels to be imperfect at everything, and to stare into a mirror that shows only your flaws. You don't know how it feels to be told by people that you're not good enough," The old man didn't utter a word for a few minutes, but then he said, "When you look into the mirror what do you see?" Angela, without acknowledging the question, turned to him and said, "I have a magical mirror, not an ordinary one."

The old man replied, "What is so magical about it?"

"It never lies," replied Angela.

"I would like to see it to believe it," said the old man, as he looked on curiously.

"Fine, I will get it tomorrow," said Angela.

The next day, she took the mirror with her, and began to look for the old man. When he saw her waiting for him, he apologised and asked her to hand the mirror over so he could have a closer look. At first he held the mirror, and then dropped it on the ground with all of his strength. Angela began to scream, "What have you done old man! I have treasured this mirror for more than 18 years, and you just broke it!"

The man once again said nothing and began to smile. Angela was going hysterical, but he stood there calmly. After some time, when Angela seemed tired, he finally broke his silence.

"My child, what do you see on the floor?"

Angela, gasping for breath and with a stare that could kill replied, "What do you see?"

The old man softly replied, "I see a girl who has been looking into a mirror of only her flaws for far too long. The mirror only reaffirms her flaws every time she looks into it. That mirror has had you in its trap!"

Angela was now trying to make sense of what the old man was suggesting.

"What do you mean, it had me in its trap?"

"Angela, what we give our attention to grows stronger and bigger. You've always looked for your flaws in that mirror, and it always reflects them back onto you. You are what you see yourself to be. The world only responds to it. My dear, we often fight a battle against the world when what we need instead is to look at the battle we're fighting within. That's the bigger battle that needs to be won. Only then can we return home, and to ourselves."

Tears rolled down Angela's cheeks as she thought of everything she had put herself through. That day she vowed to be more kind, loving, and compassionate towards herself and the world. She understood the world would take care of itself, but she had to take care of herself.

Since then, whenever she looks into a mirror, she only whispers, "I love you."

# 21

# RE-INVENTING MYSELF, OR TRYING TO
CECILE DASH

"Are you Shakira? I promise I won't tell anyone."

I glance at the 6-year-old girl in front of me, and then look from her to my daughter, and then back again to the little girl. My daughter jumps in.

"Oh no, this isn't Shakira, it's my other mom."

Confused, I leave the school yard and walk back to the car. As I put my daughter in the back, I ask her what that was all about.

"Oh nothing Mom, you just didn't understand her."

When I keep pressuring her on this topic, I finally get a, "Mom, stop it. You just emptied my bucket of happiness and it was full when I got into the car."

She leaves me speechless for the rest of the drive. Obviously, I am not Shakira. So, does that mean she needs to pretend that she has a fake Shakira mom? I am fairly sure I *did* understand her, and can't shake the feeling that my daughter made up this story to have a 'cool pretend mom.' Am I not a cool enough mom?

At dinner I take the opportunity to ask my son and daughter what it is they think I do?

My daughter is truly clear about this, "You are my mom, why, did you forget?"

My son however, scores more points, "Well you also write, help poor children, and you work sometimes."

This makes me feel a little better about myself. I can't shake the *who am I* thoughts. Who am I in their eyes? Who do I want to be? I have lost quite a few people and have attended my fair share of funerals. I tend to leave them questioning what people will say when *I* die. What will my children say? Who was I to them? I lay in bed contemplating all of these things, and feeling quite lost.

I was a workaholic; I was raised in a family where you do not sit idle and must be productive consistently. This is a very Calvinist and Dutch approach to life: don't sit around, do *it,* whatever *it* may be.

I started my first paper route when I was 13 and moved onto working on farms picking strawberries, and working in stores, restaurants, and hotels. I was busy, and that is how I liked it. If I wanted something, I worked for it. There was a time, in my teens where I wanted to become a famous model. Which teenage girl doesn't want that, right? But, modelling agencies didn't get back to me. So, when I ran out of pictures of myself to send them, I started sending family pictures in with the applications. All of a sudden, there was an interest! The photos presented six hand-some children, two of whom are adopted, and rather good - looking parents. So, without consulting those parents, we started getting bookings for a soap series, commercials, fashion shows, you name it. It was fun, but I did come to the realization that this wasn't the career for me. It was a teenage dream, one of many.

After working in hotels across Europe, I realized I loved the 24-hour operation. There was always commotion, problems to be solved, and guests to attend to. So, by the time I was 21, I decided to study hotel management. Years later, a job advertisement caught my eye: a general hospital was looking for people to implement a more hotel-like experience for their patients. I started working in the hospital, and loved it. Again, it was a 24-hour operation with fires to put out and enough challenges in a day to keep me interested. At this point, I had gotten married, had my first child, and was pregnant with my second.

When I heard of an opportunity to do a Master's degree abroad I didn't hesitate. It had the potential to lead my career forward. My husband did hesitate, however, at four months pregnant, I walked into a board room and convinced the panel that I was the right person to complete their Master's program.

They granted me the opportunity, and the University worked around my pregnancy so I could finish my degree. Which, of course, I did. So now, with a great career and two beautiful children, we decided to move abroad; to Africa to be exact.

I joked around with everyone in my midst that I was going to be this 'expat-wife' from now on, doing lunches, charity events etc. Fast forward six months, and I indeed had become that woman. I even became the president of the expat community, I didn't know how I felt about it all because I had always been the career driven type. But, because of the move, all of my usual securities were gone leaving me to question: who am I now?

I got involved in local charities and helped as much as I could. That should have been rewarding, right? To me it was not. I wanted to make a real difference. I mean I didn't need to win a Nobel peace prize or anything, but I still wanted to do something to help change the world. At the same time, it was becoming clearer to me that I also needed the applause that would normally come from a 'real' job.

There was also this immense pressure to not just do *anything*. Whatever I chose needed to be really life changing. I had the luxury to do whatever I want to do; so that something had to be mind-blowingly awesome. I felt guilty for being in such a privileged position. Maybe in another environment I would have put less pressure on myself, but living in Congo made this harder. Congo is extremely poor, and although we were living an extraordinarily rich life there, we were confronted with the severity of the conditions. Coming from Europe, I compared those conditions to those of my own upbringing, and saw an enormous difference. This was yet another thing I felt guilty about, coming from such a privileged background. I had not needed to live day by day in order to survive, like most Congolese people do.

I created this pressure on myself, and I also created way too many lists in my head that would drive any person insane. This resulted in not being able to do anything. It was like I was paralyzed. I had far too many ideas about how to change the world, the books I wanted to write, and the businesses I wanted to set up. I just couldn't prioritize anymore, because I had too much in my head. I cannot think small, and am not satisfied with small achievements. I want to tackle corruption in Africa, not just in the city where I am living, but in but in the entire continent. When I think about these types of things on a global scale, the item added into my mental to do list becomes: eliminate corruption worldwide. I then add, making healthcare available to everyone, followed by finding families for every orphan here and possibly everywhere. My relentless list goes on, and on, and on.

I started reading more about being productive, effective, and how to make life changes by following the nudges you feel inside. Well, I don't know about you, but I don't have one nudge. I have hundreds of them. Each one of them I feel passionately about, so how do I choose which one to follow? Or worse, what if I end up following the wrong one and fail miserably? Is it enough to say well, at least I tried? I needed to lower my own expectations without seeing this as a failure.

"Mom, can you help?" My youngest daughter managed to get her hair tangled into a firetruck. As I untangled her hair, the next one came: "Mom, I need help with my dress." I helped my children, and I will always help my children, but am I a bad mom for wanting more than that? Is being a mom not the most fulfilling job there is? No, not for me.

My grandmother is a very strong and forceful character, and whenever I bring up my insecurities of what it is I should do, she puts it into perspective for me: "Stop complaining, just do something! You know in my time...."

She is right, I know she is, but I am so busy trying to find my perfect, most successful path that I sometimes forget to enjoy life in the meantime. We can all agree that life is too short for that.

My daughter comes to me, yet again, "Mom, can you come to my class tomorrow? I told my teacher you are a doctor because you used to work in a hospital. So, can you come and tell my class about it?"

I laugh out loud, hug her and feel happy that in her eyes I am everything she wants me to be. I will rectify the situation with the teacher tomorrow, as I am not a doctor. Or, maybe, just maybe, I will go buy a white doctor's coat and totally rock the 'pretend doctor' act, whilst singing a Shakira song.

So, my aha-moment? My aha-moments happen all throughout my days, every day, and mostly at night. They keep changing too! So, for now I will keep collecting them until I can bundle them into one giant, 'WATCH OUT FOR THIS ONE' aha moment. That'll be my one nudge that will, or will not, change the world. Until then, I will be on a journey to find, accept, and rediscover myself.

# 22

# I WAS ALWAYS ENOUGH
### TONIA DE SA

I have struggled with self-worth and self-love for as long as I can remember. Even at three, four and five years old, I remember not feeling like I was important, seen, or enough. I have always felt invisible, lacking, and yearning for wholeness, enough-ness, and love.

I have been working on trying to love myself, heal myself, and be worthy since I was 20, and I'm now 50. But, when you are not quite sure what that looks like, it is hard to attain no matter how many books you read, courses you take, or healers/counsellors you go to.

I always felt embarrassed when gurus or friends would say, "Just love yourself." It was something foreign to me, and I didn't know the first step towards how to do that. What do they mean, *love yourself*? Sometimes I would be brave enough to ask, but they would just look at me blankly, unsure of how I could ask a question like that. "Just love yourself," sounds as bizarre to me as, "You will just know when you meet the right person." (Still waiting for that to happen too.) Suggestions came in as to how to love myself, such as bubble baths, meditation, spa days, time with friends, mirror work, and affirmations. Some of these I did, some of these I didn't do, but that elusive self- love was still out of my reach.

When I finally left a toxic marriage, which had only fed and heightened my abandonment issues and feelings of unworthiness, I hit a turning point. This finally pointed me in the direction of loving myself to the core. If I was able to be strong through this, with four young kids and a part-time minimum-wage job, it was proof enough that I not only love my kids, but myself. Gaining the strength to not only know that my children and I deserved more, but to follow through on making it happen, was a huge step in my journey towards self-love. Through independence, strength, resilience, and a beautiful tribe of supporting people, my self-love grew.

It may sound like a miracle, but it wasn't. To this day, I continue the journey towards feeling like I am enough, and choosing myself over everyone else. I am still meditating, healing, doing soul work, and surrounding myself with uplifting people. I take time to do things I love. These are all steps, but the not enough-ness has remained difficult to target and heal.

Then today, a dear friend and fellow healer asked me to repeat an affirmation and heal my deep wounds once and for all....

"I am enough." I tried this one many times, but it stays on the surface – so not this one.

"I am working to be enough." Yes, for a long time I have been, but I and am tired of chasing it, so not this one.

"I've always been enough." This resonated with me so deeply that sparks went off in my soul, sparks of excitement, freedom and truth.

I'VE ALWAYS BEEN ENOUGH.

These words uncovered a truth that was there all along. No more striving to be enough. No more listening to the lies I've told myself my entire life, including the lie that I am less than others. I am not less deserving, less pretty, less lovable, less worthy of dreams coming true, or less worthy of a life of delight.

These words liberated me. I felt free in hearing them and overcome with emotion. I wanted to cry, but a good cry because I'd finally been broken open, and I no longer needed to strive to be enough, because I always was enough, and I never knew it.

Until now.

And yes, I may forget, but this is my new mantra and I invite you to try it.

Because, if I was always enough, then you were always enough too.

# 23

# LIFE IN A FLASH

AMY LYNN

"Ok, are we ready? The camera will make a big flash. Remember, to keep your eyes opened, even if it hurts. One, two, three, here we go!!!

Amy! your eyes were closed. Let's try it again."

I tried it again, and again, and again. My heart hurt. My soul was hurt. But damn it, I could not keep my eyes open every time I saw the flash. It was too bright.

Flash 2009

"I lost myself. I think the person I was is gone forever. What do you think?"

It's ok, you are not gone. You will find her again. You will."

My best friend's sister almost died by getting shot in the face with a fishing hook in the middle of some godforsaken place in British Columbia. This cool, sweet, sexy woman chased dreams, chased adventure, and found it all. I was in awe of her. I still am. She had it all.

They said, "We knew it!! This was a bad idea. She should have never gone. How could she ever think this was a good idea?!"

I knew deep down it was awesome. She went, and she did it

all, and the hook did not kill her. She came home with a fat lip yeah, but she also came home with a killer six pack and no regrets. Her eyes were open.

Flash 2010

"Things aren't working. I don't know what is wrong exactly. But, I don't think I can keep doing this."

"Amy, all couples go through this. I don't think it would be right for you to leave. Call me anytime. Anytime."

My girlfriend worked at the school with me. Her dad was a Dean at a big University. She was tall, British, and spoke French. She was right. I was silly. I will stay. It will be ok.

Flash 2011

"My mom has to have a transplant. She might die. She will actually die if she doesn't get the surgery."

"Oh my god. What should we do? What should I do? Anything, everything. Of course. Let's do it. I love you."

I moved to Alberta in 2007. I began working as a student teacher in North Edmonton. I literally called a school (so I thought) and asked if they would accept a university student from Newfoundland as a student teacher. I had called 3 schools. One said yes. I went. I was so nervous. But I rocked it. I was working full time in the school before I even had an official teaching degree. I was on fire.

The next 4 years everything was exactly as it 'should be.' I was with my boyfriend who I met in 2005. He was working as an electrician in Northern Alberta. He was successful. He was dedicated. We had made it. Life was as it should be.

In early 2011, I was asked to be on an interview panel at my now new school. I was working in South Edmonton. Parents were shiny and pretty and rich. I was determined to make them accept me, respect me and appreciate me. And, they did. I felt myself becoming a professional. I knew what to do, how to do it and do it within the hours of eight to four. My principal (boss) also recognized this and spoke with me about having more responsibility. I knew he saw my potential and was mentoring me towards a leadership role in my field. I was ready.

My boyfriend told me about his mom. She was sick and on the other side of the country. Before he asked or said another word, I knew I was going to give up my success and my dreams. I was going to give up on me. And, I left.

My father came to meet me in June 2011 and we drove across the United States and Canada into the hardest, excruciating, and most exhausting five years of my life. I loved every second of that trip with my dad.

Flash June 2011

"Can I have your ID sir?"

"Umm yes.......here you go."

"Ever been arrested?"

"Misdemeanour."

"Dad?! What the heck??!!"

"Amy, no questions. It was a long time ago."

My dad was a BADASS. I knew it. I loved him even more. His eyes were wide open.

We drove into the beautiful land of the United Stated of America through millions and millions of flashes of blue, red and white. It was July 4th and it was breath-taking.

As we got closer to our final destination, my eyes slowly closed all the way. It was dark and lonely. The flashes were still too bright.

December 2012

There were no lights, no flashes and no glimmers of hope. I had moved into my boyfriend's family home on a big, fancy farm in Eastern Canada. We were both 28 years old and the official guardians and powers of attorney for 3 teenagers. They were my boyfriend's younger half siblings. Meanwhile, his mother was in

Edmonton awaiting a lung transplant surgery. To say that this was a clusterfuck of a situation is an understatement.

The kids loathed us. I didn't blame them.

We lived and breathed for those kids.

As time went on though, it became apparent I was doing it for the kids. He was doing it for the adoration and acceptance of his mother, his mother's love. It never came.

I don't remember a lot of specific details from this two-year time period. I do remember the emptiness, loneliness, confusion and heartache I felt grow inside me. I fought internally every day. I was so desperate to look good and do the right thing, that I completely ignored it. I told myself I was doing the right thing. Partners who love each other unconditionally go through the roughest waters together and stand by each other's sides. I firmly believed that the hard parts, like making relationships with the kids, making meals for a family of five, and driving three teenagers to this place and that, while having tough honest conversations about their mother's illness would eventually soften and become easier. Not easy, but easier. I believed together we could do it. We did. And we did it fairly well.

But the feelings never fully left. I blamed his mom, his step-dad. I thought if only they could just acknowledge how hard their son is working for them. How much he sacrificed for them. Then, we would feel good. We would feel complete. However, his mom got better, the kids grew up, we moved out. And again, I still felt like shit.

Flash 2012

My parents came to visit us during Christmas in 2012. Everything about it was awful. I felt and looked like hell. Our visit with my parents and his parents was awkward and uncomfortable. My parents were worried but had no idea what to say or do. I'd had it. I wasn't doing this anymore.

I told him. Enough! Something inside me became strong,

independent, and powerful. A very bad thing had happened. And we had stepped up to the plate and did our part. The mission was accomplished. It was time for me to fight for us, our relationship, our life. We mattered! So, we left.

I really thought that was the turning point. I felt brave and ready. I really thought I was now living on my own terms.

I was very wrong.

Flash 2013

In the spring of 2013, my partner returned to Alberta for work. This time we decided to go to a smaller town. My brother lived there. It was a compromise. Return to Alberta, but not to Edmonton. I packed up and sold the remaining life we had on the East coast and once again my dad joined me on a cross country tour to return to Alberta. On the last turn into the small town at 1:30 am we narrowly missed hitting 3 deer on the highway in fog. It felt scary, scarier than it should have.

I opened the door to the hotel room where he was staying temporarily. I instantly knew this was a bad idea. I was not listening to myself, something was not right. But how could it not? We had sacrificed and worked hard and when the job was done, we returned to our life. And we did it together. It had to be good. It had to be right. Right?

Instead, memories and anger and fear flooded into my body. I went through all of THAT and now we are in this shitty hotel room and he cannot even get up to give me a hug?

"It's late. I have to work early. I am happy you are here."

I felt the heat rising. It was a white, hot feeling of regret, confusion and fear. We were not going to return to our life. This is our life. This is it.

That night, I did not sleep. I sat wide eyed in a dingy, dark, and run down hotel room wondering what the hell had happened. I was so tired and exhausted from the trip. I left and walked out into the cold night, in the middle of nothing. I had nowhere to go and nowhere to run. I knew once and for all, unless I faced the truth, this is how life was going to be. I accepted it and felt it. I still couldn't cry.

Flash 2014

"Get up, now. You cannot lie under this fucking bus tonight. Get the fuck up."

"Leave me here. I don't care. Just go."

All of a sudden, guilt. I had no idea. I was not prepared. I was going to tell him and everyone else how sad, lonely and defeated I felt. But the brakes went on hard. I felt selfish and ashamed. How could I tell someone after this long how I felt? How could I destroy things after he suffered his moms near death, his life being torn upside down how many times in how many years??

I knew it was time to open my eyes but I was still so scared to admit the truth. I decided to shut up and put up with it.

We went through the motions for some months. We got an apartment, found jobs, excellent jobs. We attempting to buy a house. Our families and friends were proud and happy for us. Once again, we did the thing, and we did it well.

But, quietly and slowly I moved 'out,' and into the spare room. I cried myself to sleep. I knew it was time to tell the truth. My truth.

I decided to tell. I told him everything. He cried. A lot. I felt terrible. I was expecting relief and calm and strength. Instead, the guilt intensified. It was stronger than sadness, pain and loneliness.

But, something inside me knew it was right. And we parted ways. The guilt remained.

I spent a full year washing my guilt down with booze and parties. During those days I woke up many times wondering who I was and where I was. Once, I was literally under a bus. Thank god for good friends in dark times.

Flash 2015

"Hello 911, what's your emergency?"

"Hi yes, I think my boyfriend, umm friend is trying to kill himself."

"Ok ma'am. Are you safe?"

"No. I ran away, with the dog. I don't know."

"Are there weapons in the home?"

"Yes."

With that, forty SWAT rolled into town, surrounding me, the dog and the apartment. I was swooped up like a child and placed in the back of a cop cruiser. I remember thinking oh fuck. Oh fuck, my life! It was the first time I truly worried for ME. I didn't care about that guy, or his dog, as a matter of fact. I knew in that moment I had to take control of my shit and only mine.

This was truly 'the moment', a turning point, a cross-road......this was it. No more fucking around.

I watched my own life for the rest of that night like a movie. I was hidden under a blanket in the back of a cruiser. They told me to keep my head down because the media might take photos.

FLASH FLASH FLASH FLASH!!!!!

"Keep your head down!!!!"

I wanted to lift my head, but I didn't.

Eventually, the cops left, the media left. Town gossip left. And, I left too. This time not because of fear, guilt, shame, or obligation. I did it because I wanted to. I had one box in my 2008 Mazda 3. I was heading back to Edmonton. where it all began. I felt like I was flying a fucking jet. I felt fast, light and straight as an arrow. I felt like me.

As I drove, I thought of my dad and my sexy cool friend who never looked back. All the people who kept their eyes open.

I thought about how, somehow, this was different than all the other times of change. How? I don't know. But I did know, I now knew when it wasn't right.

I knew aha had happened.

Aha felt smooth, slick and sexy. It was shiny and sharp. It didn't apologize or make excuses. It didn't wake up lonely and afraid. It was confident and true.

March 2015

Aha led me to my life. The life I knew I was meant to live. I felt myself propelled forward in a way I never felt before. A raw trust in myself had developed. Call it a gut feeling, instinct, or intuition.

It had always been there. But I was afraid. It flashed its true colours many times but I wanted to do the good things, the proper things, not the TRUE things. Listening deeply led to two major circumstances in which I had to choose the truth. My truth.

Upon my return to Edmonton, I had to choose between three job offerings. I had to choose what was best for me. I chose to return to where my heart sang: being a teacher. I listened to my heart. I returned to work in a vulnerable, transient community in North Edmonton. I still work there today. I love the kids, their parents, and the community at large.

The hardest truth would be true love. I would be faced with listening to my truth more deeply than ever before.

May 2015

The day we met, the first thing he asked was if he could put his helmet on the front seat of my car. I looked at this tall, handsome man and thought to myself, you can put anything, anywhere. I wanted him.

He was strong, cool, sexy and drove a motorcycle. I was in. All in. I liked him, he liked me. It was sexy and passionate and I knew this man was someone very special.

I fell deep into him and deep into myself and deep into truth. It was magical and breath-taking. The white, hot feelings of anger and fear that I had known so well had been replaced with red hot passion and sensuality. I sank deep into him. I felt secure in his arms. He held my hand, stroked my back and made my body come alive.

June 2015

It was a warm summer night. We were laying in each other's arms. Basking in the sexiness of the moment.

"I have to be honest about something. I really like you, so much. There's something you deserve to hear."

"Ok. I am listening."

"I have a record," he said.

I began to feel the shame, guilt and expectations of everyone else. What would they think? What would they say?

But, my aha was strong.

I remembered that day on the drive with my dad. "Misdemeanour."

I love my dad so much. I trust him and respect him and when he said, "No questions." I knew what that meant and I listened to my dad.

I listened again. I listened to the man beside me. I listened to my heart. I knew I found my person. My soulmate, my love.

Sept 2015

The ride we were on in life continued. We sailed through the summer months in love. He told his family about me. I told mine about him.

But, not everything.

Fear of approval and acceptance creeped back in the little cracks. If everyone knew everything, what would they say?

I told him everything. I told him sometimes I worried about what other people think too much. And sometimes, I will let go of the great things in my life in search of approval and praise. I was embarrassed to tell him. I didn't want to believe it myself.

I knew I had found the most incredible man. I knew we were meant to be. I decided to listen again to my strongest truth. I fell completely 100% in love with him.

November 2015

Our love was strong as ever. My heart raced when I saw him, thought of him, touched him. I was floating on air. I was in a dream. Was I in a dream? Was I fooling myself?

Doubt crept in.

Was I too reliant on him? Was I losing myself to him and his strength? Had I given up myself because I was so in love? Was I becoming weak?

I listened to my heart. That deep truth inside. I knew everything we had together was deep mutual love, respect and adoration. Strength was letting someone else take the reins and trusting them fully, deeply and wholeheartedly. Strength is knowing it's okay to let someone love you, take care of you and please you. I was strong, not weak, by loving him, and letting him love me. I breathed and dropped my shoulders and rode the wave of falling deeper and deeper in love.

The Love Story

We got engaged in Cuba in December of 2016. It was a beautiful, warm evening. It was perfect. We spent the week celebrating with champagne, cake and cigars. I felt beautiful, proud, and in love.

We spent moments that week planning our wedding. We had no access to technology. We sat beside the beach discussing the details. They were simple, and exactly what we both wanted.

We decided to get married in August of 2016. I remember fully sinking into our love and our strong relationship. Wedding days can bring so many opportunities for doubt, stress and doing things for other people instead of oneself. I breathed and listened to my truth. What was important? What did we want? I knew all I wanted was a pretty dress and to finally marry the love of my life. We wanted to be together, forever.

We had the most magical day ever.

Eyes Wide Open 2020

It's been 5 years. It has been 5 years of romance and steamy nights under red lights and so much laughter with my husband.

It's been almost ten years since I first said yes to something, knowing that I wanted to say no. Ten years since the first time I remember turning my back on myself.

I sometimes think of the past five years as a do over from the five before. But, truthfully that is not how it is. I knew what the truth was. I knew what my soul was telling me. I was simply nervous.

As the years went on, I developed courage and strength. When I was ready, I opened up. I am now surrounded by the love of my husband, and raw, true friendships accompanied by the deepest sense of self I never could have never imagined.

Listen to your strong, powerful self. Even if it is just a flash, the truth will shine through.

# 24

# A DANCER'S EDUCATION

STEPHANIE KNOWLER

The same week that I walked the stage to accept my Master's degree parchment, I handed my resignation in at the prestigious private school I had been teaching at for seven years. It was a bold decision: one that came with a flurry of marital debate, incredible apprehension, and feelings of major regret. My husband texted me from the bleachers during the ceremony, saying: "Congratulations. You finally got your Master of Education, and you quit your teaching job." Talk about a whirlwind of emotions.

Achieving that Master's degree was a feat in and of itself: I found out I was pregnant two months into the start of my program. We had been trying, but did not expect to get pregnant that quickly. Isn't that always how it goes? So exactly nine months later, and after finishing all my course work for my thesis based program, I applied for my first maternity leave from my research. I returned to work full time when my son turned a year old, and continued my research late at night, often with a baby sleeping in my arms.

Exactly one and a half years after that, I came to discover that the universe loves to throw you curve balls when you get too cocky. I found out I was pregnant again in October, much to our excitement! I've always been one to brag about my multitasking capabilities, and true to form, three months later at 21 weeks I discovered that I was carrying identical twins! This immediately thrusted me into the high- risk category, and shortly thereafter I was put on bedrest. I applied for an emergency leave from my university program. Surprise twins tend to allow for that. Surprise twins, I might add, that decided to make their arrival at 32 weeks. Six (wild) months after the girls were born, I continued my research. I have photos of me in bed, breast-feeding the girls to sleep on their giant pillow while my toddler is asleep beside me in just his pull up. My laptop is open on my lap, and my ear buds are in so I can listen to my interviews. I'm giving my husband a goofy two thumbs up. What a photo.

Honestly, it was a shit show of utter chaos. The blessing in disguise was that exclusively breastfeeding twins meant that I literally never slept, and thus was able to stay up writing into the wee hours of the morning. I am quite confident that I spent over 200 hours transcribing the 30+ interviews that I conducted for my thesis. And, that was just the transcription part. When I finally submitted my thesis for completion, and defended it in February of 2017 (a few years later than planned), I insisted that my five year old and my almost two year old twins attend my grad photos. The result was the most ridiculous and yet memo-rable graduation photo ever. I have one toddler pulling at my cap tassel, the other grabbing at my flower prop, and my son, laughing hysterically while covering his face while I held him in place. My husband was grinning from ear to ear. That photo is framed and takes a place of honour on my china cabinet to remind me that I can do so many hard things, and often all at once.

Anyways, I digress...

...kind of. Reflecting back on all of this, it must have looked like complete mayhem to an outsider. I mean really, it was. That being said, I never questioned any of it. I was determined to finish what I had started, and achieve top marks while doing so: even with three kids. And, so I did.

And then, as you know, I quit my job.

Why did I quit my teaching career? Well, I resigned from my teaching job to focus on my small business and to raise my young children. In 2007 my two younger sisters and I founded a children's dance studio. Because we grew up dancing, it was a childhood dream of ours. Together, we envisioned creating a safe and respectful place for children to learn dance through proper technique and education. Having developed so many positive relationships through dance ourselves, it was important to us that we provide an opportunity for a supportive dance community to exist. At the time it was just a small gig on the side of university courses and teaching careers. With our team of amazing faculty, we grew our small business from a 25 student, very part time operation, to a thriving 300 dancer studio. Not to mention that we accomplished this in a city saturated with so many dance studios. We were in our prime, and then the pandemic began. And, like all small businesses around the world, we took a major blow and were forced to adapt our business immediately. I could write an entire book about the past ten months, but will save that for another anthology. I want to talk more about finding myself and my purpose in my business.

Two years ago, my sister and I started working with a business coach. To be honest, I was skeptical at first, but encouraged to do so by our graphic designer, who I think very fondly of. The recommendation was to book a discovery call with our graphic designer's coach. We were SO ready to take our business to the 'next level.' So, we met with her and it was an immediate connection. My sister and I didn't even need to look at each other for permission or agreement before we committed to a six month coaching program. What we didn't realize at the time was just how important it would be to have someone bring a new perspective, fresh ideas, and innovation to our growing business. She helped us flush out our values and vision for our studio. These were things we contemplated previously, but had never before put words to. It was exhilarating to put fresh paint on an entity that we had spent countless hours investing ourselves into. The result was a whole new level of growth. We then went on to join two different mastermind groups; which also helped us direct our vision and refine our purpose. I cannot say enough positive things about growing a business in a united community of like-minded individuals; collaboration over competition, as the saying goes.

Throughout this entire time, I started to experience what every good female does: imposter syndrome. Here I was, a highly educated woman with three degrees and four young kids. I was literally juggling diaper changes with business calls, folding the never disappearing 'laundry mountain,' while also leading a team of 14 dance educators. I kept reminding myself that I chose this; I wanted to be home to support my kids, while also focusing on my business. There were going to be some days that were truly overwhelming with 'kid stuff' and other days involving me being at the studio all day. I mean, really, I had the best of both worlds: I would send the other three to school, and work from home while the baby napped or played on the floor. And, once I'd put the kids to bed after books and cuddles, I'd work for a few hours in the evening. Unfortunately, I was not satisfied. I kept telling myself I was a fraud, an imposter. I looked around at the other studio owners who had university degrees in dance. I did not - I have an undergraduate degree in religious studies. I saw former professional dancers starting their new studios. I hadn't ever danced professionally either. (I am going to go ahead and admit that my time performing with a Ukrainian dance ensemble was nothing close to a professional dance career.) I didn't have a business degree, so who was I to think I could run a business? I was no longer a teacher, so I convinced myself that I could no longer call myself a professional. Sure, I have a Master's degree in Education, but I tried persuading myself that my focus on social justice issues was irrelevant to my business, knowing deep down that it actually serves many areas. I was lost and unsure of what my focus should be, what my goals were, and what I wanted out of all of this...

Then one day, I literally had an "aha" moment. I remember it so clearly. I was working on some goal setting and social media related posts pertaining to our studio pillars: Learn, Connect, Inspire. We had spent countless hours refining these and decided that the intent of every decision should relate back to these three elements. I was reflecting on the 'connect' pillar and how I related to it. I may not have had a professional dance career, or a degree in dance, but I grew up dancing, and love to dance. Albeit, I may not dance as well in this maturing body as I once did. Regardless, so many of my closest and lifelong friends are from my time dancing. Even now, through my studio, I have forged some amazing friendships as a studio owner, teacher and parent. Dance is what connects us. Even more importantly, I adore children and have always had a very natural way of connecting with them. My mom used to call me a 'kid magnet' because wherever I went I attracted children, and this is still true today. I have been working with children for over 25 years in a multitude of roles and through that time have developed a very thorough understanding of child development. I understand what is age appropriate, and how to form positive and respectful relationships with kids of all ages. Furthermore, since researching and reading is truly my jam, I realized that my Master's degree in Educational Research actually compliments my role as the director and owner of a child-centred business.

As well, my background in social justice issues are complimentary of this position.

I spent many months last year reading about and attending virtual conferences on the philosophy of play in children's learning. I then developed a framework for preschool dance unique to our studio, and then focused on bringing attention to this uniqueness. Not only that, once I started to realize just how clearly the emphasis was on education at our studio, the more I recognized that people came to us for that reason. Whether it was parents seeking a dance studio for their children, or a new teacher looking for a position, the thing that attracted them to our door was our education, experience and knowledge. It actually turns out that I am no imposter; I am a highly qualified educator and business owner with a clear purpose and vision. I can confidently claim that I have an innate ability to connect with most children. Connection is, without a doubt, what drives our business and what I bring forward as a business owner. Ultimately, a successful business reflects the values of the owner, does it not? At the very least, it should make it easier to market and sell the purpose and vision...

Will I ever go back to teaching? That is really hard to say. It was, and is, part of who I am. I will always be a teacher, whether I am in an actual classroom or not. What I do know is that being a leader, a creator, an innovator, and a decision maker is in my blood. Second only to my children, my business is my joy. It is, both literally and figuratively, what gets me out of bed in the morning (and keeps me up at night!). All of my education, as well as these past events and experiences, have led me here, and I am privileged to be able to share my passion with others.

# 25

# THE HERO AND THE DRAGON
SHARANA ALI

I would be the perfect mom. I knew it. I mean, how hard could it be?

I believed that the perfect mom was the cookie cutter mom: Joan Cleavers or Angela Bower.

As a mom, I wouldn't just have a great job, I'd cook and clean as well. I would have a well behaved and dressed baby. My loving husband would be tall, strong, and hilarious. Our huge home would always be tidy and a freshly cooked meal would always be in preparation. The most perfectly baked chewy chocolate chip cookies would be on the counter.

It's quite something when these are your dreams as early as five years old.

Frankly, these were the examples I saw around me. This was the home I lived in, the movies I watched, the stories I read, and the storylines of the games I played. How could I not want that happily ever after?

And so, I chased it.

I listened and was the good girl. I didn't break the rules, and I wasn't disrespectful. I went to school and got a university degree, followed by a reputable job in a steady industry. I got married, had the beautiful home, as well as great friends and an amazing family unit. I manifested the societal equation that was supposed to result in happiness and perfection; but I was broken.

I was exhausted. I didn't recognize the shell of a woman I was internally, because externally, I had it all together, complete with a plastered smile on my face.

And then, I had my daughter.

In that very moment that I saw those double blue lines, I could feel the weight of the world on my shoulders. I was going to be responsible for another human being, and I didn't even know who I was, what I stood for, or what I wanted out of life. Yet, I filled all of society's check boxes.

Inside of that woman who looked like she had and did it all, was a broken human craving love, acceptance and attention. I questioned if society had failed me, or if I had simply failed myself for prioritizing society over myself.

This pregnancy was my dream answered. My daughter would eventually serve to be my agent of change; because, at the time, I couldn't be that for myself.

My pregnancy, physically, could have been used as a medical textbook example. There was no chaos, nor unusual aches, pains or worries. But mentally, I was a volcano waiting to erupt. I was constantly emotionally and mentally alone, while physically living with someone.

The support I needed and deserved was not there.

There was no love, excitement or happiness. Instead, I lived with shame, guilt and a need to stay small. My priority was ensuring that my partner was comfortable.

For a year and a half after having my daughter, I existed in a silent world. I did everything myself, and kept so much grief and hurt inside. At this time, my partner and I separated. I could breathe again and continued to for a year until I decided to give my marriage a second chance. Why? Because I still craved that white picket fence life for my child, and because there was commitment to change. I so wanted what the world saw as a 'whole family.'

It didn't last.

I was unhappy. I no longer cared. It was too late for the effort. The verbal cuts were far too deep, and developed over far too many years. I didn't deserve the lies, games and hurt. And more importantly, it wasn't the life I wanted for my child. Today, my daughter is 4 years old, and I'm a healing, divorced, single mother combating narcissistic abuse and its lifelong effects on us. I'm working through anxiety, advocating for my beliefs, and discovering my truth.

And you know what? I'm the happiest I've been, and so is my daughter.

In order to find myself, I had to give life; which in turn, showed me the life I wanted to give myself. And, I am the perfect mom after all, except that it looks nothing like the stories I witnessed or read about. I'm perfect only for the life my daughter and I have built together, and I wouldn't be suited for any other motherhood spot. It's far from glitzy, glamorous, and gorgeous, but it's perfect for us.

Motherhood is emotional, excruciating, rewarding, exciting, scary, fulfilling, lonely, empowering, motivating and an absolute tornado. And yet, it's exactly what I always wanted. For me to realize what my actual fairytale is and should feel like, I needed to become my own damn hero: a single mom that refused to give up just because it was the easier option.

The choice to become a single mom was the most emotionally draining, heart wrenching, freeing decision I ever made.

Our house isn't spick and span, and there's no white picket fence. I am both parents at the same time while my daughter is with me. We have both moments are pure insanity and complete bliss, often hours apart.

Unconventionally, I am the mother that has extremely open conversations with her child. I heavily value her opinions, choices and decisions. She is my equal. I don't claim to know more simply because I'm the adult. We are learning and unlearning together. We talk about it all: no emotion, question or topic is off the table.

I'm the mom who leads through emotion over following what experts, friends and family members are doing or advising. What is right for the emotional health of my daughter and I comes before the advice of my mother, experts with impressive accolades, or what mommy123 has to say on the internet.

I have a glass of wine at night, drop the eff bomb regularly, and am sarcastic, messy, loud and inappropriate at times. I dance down grocery store aisles wildly. My daughter is fueled by love, autonomy, mutual respect and chicken nuggets. I make a point of showing her and proving to myself that you don't have to fit in a box; you're allowed to be happy on your own terms. There is beauty in being different, and every fibre of your being has worth. I want her to know her value, without relying on society or a fairytale's depiction of what her life should look like. I want her to create the terms of her own fairytale, where she can be both the hero and the dragon to be slayed.

Ultimately, I want her to be happy; because once upon a time I was not, until she came to be.

# 26

# HEALING FROM THE HEART

DANIELLE THOMPSON

It all started sometime after completing high school and finishing my aesthetic certificate. I began noticing that clients wanted more than aesthetics. They wanted deep healing below the surface. This realization led me to taking my level one reiki training. I began to do self–healing, as well as healing for family and friends; but at the time I didn't step fully into it.

Eventually I met the man I was going to marry and we dated for a few years before deciding to have our first child. This is where the journey really began.

The pregnancy went well other than some small common issues, and we believed we were having a healthy and strong baby boy. The delivery most certainly was not one of my finest moments, but Matt and I got through it and welcomed Stanley into the world.

Life as new parents began just like it does for most other people. And then, BANG! At three and a half weeks old, baby Stanley became very fussy. One afternoon, we had just been out running errands and getting his birth certificate. I arrived home with him and began to take him out of his car seat. His clothes were soaked, and as I lifted him up he began to bleed from the mouth. My first thought was that he must have gotten upset and bit his lip or something. Then I realized that without teeth that would be very unlikely. I grabbed some Kleenex and began wiping the blood away. After it soaked through two tissues in mere seconds, we were off to the emergency room. Once we arrived to our small-town hospital, the nurse took one look at us and sent us directly into the operating room. Within minutes all staff members on shift entered the room and I immediately was on the phone with Matt urging him to get to the hospital as soon as possible. I won't go into the specifics, but it was a difficult and excruciating time.

Ultimately, two major things occurred. We found out something was irregular with Stanley's heart and that he was bleeding from the lungs, most likely due to his body going into shock. He had become critical, and we waited for the children's hospital transport team for over two hours as he fought for his new born life. I learned then that someone under ten pounds cannot be taken in an air ambulance. Waiting for transport to stabilize him enough to take him into the children's hospital is a time that will never leave me mind. How did this little human survive losing almost all his blood, being septic, and lethargic? In the moment I never thought about this, but today I am so grateful that I had the connection and ability to support that tiny human and his life force in a battle for his life.

Once he was fully assessed, he was determined to be *critically* stable, but stable. We waited for him to build strength for yet another test of his life, heart surgery. Stanley fought through that too. Today, he is the strongest and most heart loving child and boy that I have ever met. We faced numerous other challenges along the healing journey and due to the surgery. But, just like he fought initially, he fought through all of them and knocked them out cold!

Those experiences were eye opening, life changing, and definitely my face- first push back into the healing powers within. But, as is often the case, the universe seemed to believe that I hadn't received the message loud enough. Matt and I were waiting before even considering to have a second child. We asked professionals about the risks and possibilities of medical concerns. We were told the chances were very low or none at all. This lead us to begin the journey of conceiving a second. Before long, we were expecting.

Because of our history with Stanley, the medical world was all over testing and checking the unborn baby for any signs of concern. Much to our dismay, they found Stanley's same condition as well as two additional holes in her heart. As if that weren't enough, I had a sub chronic hemorrhage which made me even more high risk. It turned our world upside down once again. We needed to move to be close to the hospitals, and it hit me emotionally, mentally, and physically. I felt like the world was against me, and like I had done something wrong to deserve this. I asked WHY every single day. I got lost in all of that.

And then, just as we were pushing through, the universe threw its third pile on us which absolutely crumbled me. Here I was, pregnant and high risk and now my husband, Matt, became bed ridden with sickness. Seriously? For a month he continuously deteriorated. What was wrong with him? My mind was consumed with WHY, WHY, WHY? I was angry and resentful. Once Matt was critical, they finally found that he had a tumour blocking his entire colon. Hello Colon Cancer; not nice to meet you.

After he underwent surgery to remove the tumour and organ parts, he began eight cycles of chemotherapy. Chemo is a beast of its own. The side effects made it difficult for Matt to function and he couldn't attend many medical appointments with me due to sickness. And because of the pregnancy, I couldn't attend his treatments with him. I was on the rocks, down and out, and just so filled with anger.

During this time, I had a friend and reiki master reach out to offer me the opportunity to complete my level two training. Another friend then connected me to someone for my Master's training. At this point, many of my healer friends were sending distance healing and I felt like I had nowhere else to go but forward. I grabbed the life support thrown at me, and completed both trainings within a month of each other. The courses awoke something inside of me and gave me an outlet to release anger in a safe and healthy place.

I started doing self-healing daily, and distance healing for my husband. I continued to ask other healers to send distance healing during these times as well.

We were all doing better, day by day. Matt was still under-going chemotherapy when baby Rose was born. We had our baby girl. So many people began telling me that we had the dream family, complete with a boy and a girl. Calling us a *dream family* seemed a touch disconnected considering everything.

Rose was born and taken immediately for evaluation and monitoring. I saw her every day in the hospital, but all I could do was hold her and be there for her days old soul while she was poked, tested and checked hourly. She held her ground though, and beat the odds set out for her. She was expected to undergo the same surgery her brother had had; but then we were told that she might not not need surgery at all. Her body began healing her heart itself ...for the most part.

But Rose wasn't done with the medical world yet. Oh no, that wouldn't be our style. She started having seizures. I was abso-lutely terrified as I didn't know much about them or what was happening. Due to them, there were more hospital visits. We even started a competition with her brother for who would take an ambulance the most. Rose was finally diagnosed with

Epilepsy and given a medication to help. Today, she is getting a very minimal dose and we've been without an episode for months. Additionally, Matt has been cancer free for over a year now, and is slowly rebuilding his strength: body, mind, and soul.

Recently, people started asking me how we got through it all. Many are in disbelief, and unsure of how it was possible. I don't know. I just say that we had to. We did what we had to do in each moment.

Things started to settle. Everyone become stable, as the medical professionals say. Stabilization then gave us time to reflect. Matt and I began talking one day, and he said:

*"Do you know what got us though all of this? Do you know what got us through three out of four of our family having life threatening concerns? What got us through, is that you have a gift. You are a healer. How else do you explain it?"*

This is when it hit me. No one had answers for us as to why it all happened, or how everyone miraculously overcame it all. But Matt made a good point. I am the only one in the family without medical concerns, and I am the one who is connected to the life force and the powers it contains. I was the constant for all three of them, through it all. I had had to strengthen my own body, mind, and soul during those times just to get through it, or so I thought anyways. Maybe my ability to manage it all was a sign from the universe that I am to heal my loved ones, that I am here to empower their bodies, minds, and souls.

This realization hit me like a freight train as I am not the person to praise myself. But damn, when the universe has a message and a path for you, it probably couldn't become more clear than after enduring all of that.

I started doing energy sessions and then began to realize how misinformed the world is about the powers we contain within, and how the medical world and holistic world don't need to be in competition. My mission became to empower other women and educate them along the journey. It has evolved over the last year and a half, but the mission has become increasingly more clear and focused. My connection with the universe, and my higher powers and guides has become stronger than I ever could have imagined. The question of WHY is no longer within me. The anger has been healed and released. It is clear that enduring it all illuminated my purpose on this planet. It helped me become aware daily of my power.

Energy healing is a lifestyle for my family. Both kids are extremely connected and their souls are developing along with their bodies and minds. Matt has seen the power connected to life forces, and together we create a home and life filled with all aspects of healing.

I focus on guiding other women to heal themselves and empower them through education, so that they may bring healing into their minds, souls, bodies and homes.

# 27

# AH-HA MOMENTS

SAMANTHA TUFTS

*A daughter. A girlfriend. A student.*

Those were the only words I could think of when my second-year writing professor asked me to describe who I am. I always thought I would be more than that. I strived to be more than that. Yet, I was finding myself always falling a little short of my expectations. I had this vision of who I would be going into college: *ultra-confident, outgoing, high-achieving, super fit and healthy, and student of the year.*

I gained 20 pounds, had average grades, and sat in the corner for every class praying the professor wouldn't look my way. This didn't change until the winter of year three. I was not doing well in school, and felt unintelligent and ashamed of myself for not upholding what I had envisioned for these years. I was at a stage where the stress was too much to handle. I was crying myself to sleep every night and my grades paralleled my feelings: low and less than average. I felt like I had zero control over my emotions and I let that affect my relationships. I wanted to be more. I wanted to be great in *my own* way. I put pressure on myself to be perfect and look perfect; meanwhile, I was getting lost in everything that went wrong with my plan. I was comparing myself to everyone in my class and online, believing that I could never measure up. But, weren't these supposed to be the best years of my life? Weren't these supposed to be the years I would never forget?

After months of crying daily and telling myself I was going nowhere in life, I decided to take control. It was a process of re-learning who I was. After four months of weekly therapy, I was feeling the best I had ever felt. I was going to the gym four times a week and feeling stronger than ever. This is when I began to put more positive effort into my school work. My relationships started to change for the better and I just felt good. Therapy helped me own my strengths and accept my weaknesses.

During therapy, I had that "ah-ha" moment that most young women, experiencing the struggles of school while trying to mature, believe will never come to them. I definitely thought it was never going to happen for me. What I did believe at the time, was that that I had peaked in high school and I was never doing the right thing with my life. But in March of 2019, after months of therapy and working on my mental and physical health, I started my dream blog. I always had these amazing ideas and visions of who I could be but never the confidence to just freaking own it.

*A writer. A fitness lover. A creator. A confident woman. A leader. An ally. An independent woman. A friend. An ever-evolving badass who can handle anything. A daughter. A girlfriend. A student.*

My blog was 'the more' for me. It had taken me years to get the confidence to create it and put myself out there for people to judge. I had always wanted my own blog, and a place to create content to help other women, but I never thought my writing was good enough or that I was pretty enough to be a 'blogger.' After therapy, I decided to do what makes me happy and not focus on the opinions of other people or the lies I told myself in my lowest moments. Some days I still can't believe that I just did it. I'm currently still figuring out my life because after college, I have a lot of changes to come. I'm taking it day by day. At some point, I realized that my grades were never bad, but I let the weight of them swallow me when I didn't reach my high-achieving expectations. I was doing well all along, but wouldn't allow myself to be happy if I didn't align with my perceived idea of 'perfection.'

The person I was one year ago is not the same person that I see in the mirror today, and I couldn't be happier with the person I have become. The confidence I found from supporting and taking care of myself motivated me to also start writing a fictional book and work towards my dream of becoming a published author. Loving yourself, giving yourself grace, and believing in your personal power has a domino effect in life.

I am learning how to control the negative emotions that pull me back to who I was before, and by doing this I am redefining who I am. My "ah-ha" moment came from the lowest point in my life. Paradoxically, this was the point where I was 'supposed to' be happy, carefree, and working towards my perfect career. I just couldn't live up to those stereotypes of a young college student, but that's okay with me now. I am figuring out what I want for my life on *my* terms, not on what I think other people will approve of. I have maintained my passion for writing and blogging, and I make those things a priority for me because they make me feel good. For students, it's difficult not to let grades determine your worth and abilities. We are told that certain grades are good while others are below average or lacking. Young women have to deal with numbers every day: the number on the scale, the number on our clothes, the number of people we have been with, the number of calories we eat. It can become overwhelming, but it can never own us unless we let it.

I would like my experience and words to be a sign. If you're reading this, no matter if you're 25 or 55, you are enough to be more. I am enough to be more. Women are enough to be more no matter what society or our fears want us to believe. Be open to support, be open to growth, and let yourself be the best version of you. There doesn't always need to be a low moment, just a moment where things start to shift from where you are now to where you can be even more. I hope all women experience that "ah-ha" moment that allows them to find their more, whatever that may be.

# 28

# DESTINED TO DANCE

RENATA PAVREY

The audience watches in rapt attention, mesmerized by the energetic and expressive *Shiv Tandav* – a recreation of the divine dance performed by Shiva, described as the source of the cycle of creation, preservation, and dissolution. Lord Shiva is *Nataraja*, the god of dance. His *Tandav* is a pictorial allegory of the five principal manifestations of eternal energy: creation, preservation, illusion, destruction and salvation. The *Shiv Tandav* is her favourite piece of the *Odissi* repertoire. Because of the strength, stamina, agility, grace, and elegance required to perform it, she believes it to be the epitome of a dancer's abilities. The show goes on, one enthralling performance after another, each one leaving the audience asking for more. And, when the curtains are drawn, the applause is thunderous in its rhythm.

Exiting the auditorium, still soaking in the admiration and praise showered on her, she realizes she is soaking equally in the rain that has started pouring down. The glare of the oncoming headlights blinds her, and before she can react she is thrown off, the car itself has slid off the road, and rammed into the pavement. She can see glaring lights, hear voices all around – no sight or sound she can quite pick up clearly. She tries to get up, but realizes her right leg has been wedged between the vehicle and a wall. Or at least what was her leg. Seems more like a mass of bone and skin from what she can see. The lights get even more glaring, the voices distant. And then there's darkness, and silence.

When she regains consciousness, she notices the drab colours of the hospital walls and the peculiar smell of the ward. She tries to sit up but fails again and again. She had failed to sit up somewhere else before. The night of the accident dawns on her. She fumbles for the bedcover. The revelation is all beneath it. The nurse rushes in and comes to her aid. Her parents follow. Questions are asked. Answers are given, albeit hesitantly. The leg was severely crushed...too much blood loss...infection had set in...it had to be cut off to save her. All that's left of what used to be a leg is a stump just above the knee. She remembers Shiva. She thinks of the small statue of *Natraja* on her bedside table at home. Dance is her only religion. Now what?

The doctors are encouraging. But what do they know of dance? All they strive for is for her to be mobile. The wheelchair is drawn in. Crutches are brought in for her to try out. Assurances are given that these will be temporary; she will be receiving prostheses. Word had been spread about her being a professional dancer, and a good samaritan had offered to fund the prostheses. But that will take a while to construct, hence the crutches for now.

Life goes on. It went on without her, and will keep going on whether she chooses to partake in it or not. Dance was her life. Life has surely ended, she believes. Her physiotherapy treatments are on – the rest of the body still needs to be mobile enough or even the functional parts will suffer muscle wasting. Her arms and shoulders need to get stronger to balance on the crutches. Her pelvis needs to be aligned since all her body weight shifts to the left. Who would have thought one leg made all that difference? The rest of the body is intact, but the missing part always seems to be the most crucial one.

Her dance mates come to visit. She notices a change in behaviour. She's not competition anymore – the ones who envied her earlier appear sorry now. Could that be guilt? Did they want for this to happen to her? Others are indifferent; visiting to be polite. She won't amount to much in the dance studio now; why waste time here? Rather spend that time rehearsing. The visits reduce to calls, the calls reduce to messages, and then the messages are sent via others. The months pass and that horrific monsoon day is forgotten by everyone but her.

Months pass and she receives her new artificial leg – that starts from just above the knee. More physiotherapy. Now she needs to learn how to fit it, move it, move with it. The therapist is encouraging; she is making good progress, she will be walking fine in no time. But how is "walking fine" sufficient? Nothing is sufficient when there is no dance. The therapist reiterates – we all need to start from somewhere. Even as toddlers, we start by crawling, then hoist ourselves up taking support of anything or anyone nearby, taking tentative steps, hobbling forward gradually, then the pace picks up. We fall ever so often, but we still keep at it. She reminds her that she wasn't born performing on stage. All those little steps as a baby added up to finally make her the athletic dancer that she was. Similarly, the artificial limb is going to require those tentative steps – it is just about starting to walk. They still need to work on her pelvic alignment. Now that she has given up the crutches for the artificial leg, her body has to be taught to put weight on the new leg – balancing equally on both limbs. Though she can physically see the leg, she can't feel it touching the ground. She fails to understand where she lies in space – the mind plays tricks at times. The pair of them have work to do – balance, stability, proprioception – the mind and body both need to be worked on.

At home, she spends time with *Nataraja*. She had performed the *Shiv Tandav* at her last show, almost a year now since the accident. The God she prayed to left her with this impediment. But isn't that what the *Tandav* is? Creation with destruction – He who gives, also takes. She pays a visit to her dance class. If not her (ex) co-dancers, her dance teacher had always been in touch. Everything takes time, she had said. Whether a week, a month, a year or more, the dance school would always be open to her. Her teacher was more of a mother and mentor, than a mere instructor. A year gone by with no dancing. She had never spent a day or two without dancing her whole life. She enters the class hesitantly. The teacher is as warm and welcoming as if she had never left. She attempts a *namaskar* (Heels together, toes and knees turned out to the sides, squatting on the toes – a form of respect to Mother Earth on which one dances, failing to realize she had never practised it with the artificial leg, causing her to promptly lose balance and topple over. The dancers laugh, taunts are passed, maybe she should just walk/limp/hobble back out.

The teacher calls her to the side, offers her a chair. She refuses to sit through dance. Who does that? Why come to the studio if one has to sit? The teacher sends a few of the beginner students from the children's batch towards her. She has to teach them the *hasta mudras* (hand gestures). You asked who sits through dance? Who says a dancer uses only the legs to dance? The Odissi dance incorporates the eyes, neck, waist, arms, wrists, fingers – you have all of those functioning properly, plus one fully functional original leg, and a fully functional artificial one – all that needs to be done is make them work together. The day is spent teaching the children the hand movements, formulating stories with each *mudra* – just as she had done as a beginner student herself, all those years ago. They begin with the *asamyukta hasta mudras* – the single hand gestures. *Mayura* – the peacock, *Ardhachandra* – the half moon, *Padmakosha* – the lotus flower, *Simhamukha* – the lion's face . There are twenty eight single hand gestures in the classical dances. The children learn the meanings of each, how to curl their fingers and form each one, and weave stories with their hands. With years of dance experience and numerous choreographies, the movements were so thoroughly engrained in her that they became mechanical after a point. Teaching these children was so refreshing, dissecting each finger movement, straightening them out, curling them in, isolating them, and bringing them together. From single hand gestures, they moved to double hand gestures – *samyukta hasta mudras* - using both hands together, comprising twenty three types in all. *Anjali* – salutation, *Shankha* – the conch shell, *Matsya* – the fish, *Garuda* – the eagle - more stories gesticulated.

Beginners have a lot to learn – not just the technical aspects of dance, but also unleashing creativity. That is why classical dance is as difficult as it is. It is not just about learning a piece of choreography in three months, performing on stage, and forgetting once it is done. Classical dance is a way of life – it requires dedication and discipline. These children will not even receive their costume and accessories till the second year of training – the traditional *Odissi* attire, comprising the *saree*, headgear and jewellery has to be earned. And she has been put in charge of helping them earn it. From hand movements they move on to eye movements – *drishti bheda*. *Pralokita* – moving the eyeballs from side to side, *Anuvritta* – moving them up and down; we use such movements in our daily lives but might not have identified with their names. There are eight types of eye movements as described in the *shastras*. *Shirobheda* follows – the head movements – nine in total. *Udhvahitam* – looking up, *Adhomukham* – looking down; head positions to express a particular *bhava* or feeling. The neck movements are called the *grivabheda* – an integral part of the classical dances, and are of four types. The torso bends and rotations are the most critical movements of *Odissi* dance, that lend gracefulness to the body movements.

And she has achieved this sitting in the chair. All these months later, helping out the little ones (and some adult beginners as well), who would have thought one could dance without even having to stand? Years of being an able bodied individual, she took all this for granted. Her definition of a dancer was being able to jump around, bound across the stage, and perform high-energy sequences with vigorous movements. By entrusting these new students to her care, her teacher took her back to her own student years, when she was equally clueless, but learned step by step. All classical dancers learn the same way – hand gestures, eye movements, head and neck movements, torso bends, followed by footwork and steppings – the foundational movements for any *Odissi* dancer. Classical dance is not about athleticism, but grace, elegance, strength and endurance. One can express these things even while being stationary. Her favourite dance, the *Tandava* itself, has seven types depending on when and how Shiva performs it.

Without mentioning it directly, her dance teacher is helping her re-learn her own dance by teaching the new students. By watching the older students, she becomes more aware of the *abhinaya* of different sequences – dances she always did but had focused more on the physicality than spirituality at the time. She learns to be more tuned into the expressive form of dance – how to gather the attention of the audience by making them one with the dance. The audience should not just appreciate the dancer, but also the dance. The dancer is dance after all. How many times had she performed just for applause? Wasn't that the music she danced to? But was that what she was taught as a young dancer? She believed dance was her religion, but was she dancing for herself or for the admiration of others? Her time teaching the younger ones and observing the elder ones make her more reflective into her own past life as a dancer. A performer can learn by being an observer. By putting oneself in the seat of the audience, one can learn how to empathize with being offstage, in turn learning to connect better when onstage. All these reflections change how she sees herself as a dancer. There's so much more she can learn and do. Now that she's starting from scratch, all she needs to do is put herself in the beginner's seat. This past year and a half since the accident, she has been comparing herself with her past life as a dancer. But in retrospect, she was more of a performer than a dancer. For dancing is what is within oneself, even if it might not be perfect for others. And when what is within oneself is pure and yields joy, that is what gets reflected on to others. Yes, she will start from the beginning – every *mudra*, every neck tilt, every torso bend will be focused in – no matter how small the movement. For it is the little movements practised regularly that build the foundation and aid the larger movements in the future.

She sets her mind to her own practise as well. With the little *Nataraja* statue as witness, she religiously practices at home whatever she had taught her students that day. Taking support of a wall, she cautiously bends into a half squat, preparing for the *namaskar*, and continuing holding on for support. She lowers herself further into a full squat, trying to retain her centre of balance. With the wall for support, she can successfully manage the basic homage to Mother Earth. She just needs to keep at it, and soon enough she should be able to accomplish the movement without any support.

The dance institute is preparing for its upcoming annual

day. In her pre-accident years, she would perform multiple solo pieces. This time it is a small role in a group sequence. After a long time, she will be rehearsing with other dancers. Her role in the piece is miniscule, but she helps with the entries and exits of the other performers, observing the other stronger dancers practice. Strangely, she does not miss being them. Her months of teaching the children and re-learning her own dance have taught her to be the best she can be: no comparison with others. Just learning to grow each day, and be stronger and better than she was the day before. The annual function is a stellar success. *Odissi* is a niche dance form and does not generally have a large audience. But the ones who came were very pleased with what they saw and experienced. This time the applause she receives is not for herself, but for the whole dance company. She begins to appreciate the feeling of team spirit. It takes each performer to make the show a success. Even in a group sequence, each one's contribution is vital. However tiny the part, even if one person misses a beat, the entire performance gets affected. She used to be so focused on her own choreographies and dances earlier, without any concern about what the rest of the troupe might have been doing. Realization dawns – it was never about her; they all put in their efforts for the show. It is the team that makes the individual stronger, and each individual that adds to the team strength in turn. We learn and grow from each other. The applause for her seemingly bit role, is the best she has ever heard.

Dance continues. Life goes on. Her little *Nataraja* statue laying an observant eye, she keeps up with her physiotherapy exercises, dance stretches and basic movements. She increases her awareness about her centre, becomes more balanced, able to move efficiently and transfer weight on both legs. She feels stronger. But more than the physicality, her dance has turned more expressive. She learns to showcase her grace and elegance rather than athleticism.

She is painting out *alta* – the bright red dye to adorn her palms and feet. The classical dances depict stories of various gods and goddesses, and hence *alta* forms a significant part of the Vedic sixteen bridal adornments, also known as the *solah shringar*. The radiant red liquid looks striking on both feet. No comparisons between the real leg and the artificial limb – they will both be decorated. She ties on her *ghunghroos*, one by one – the melodic ankle bells. A sound so pure, it is held close to the heart, though wound on the feet – something her teacher had said to her. Her school has been invited to perform at the opening ceremony of a function. She steps on to the stage when it is her turn. A solo sequence – the *megh pallavi* – her favourite among all the *pallavis*. The *pallavi* is a pure dance item in *Odissi* that implies elaboration and exposition, not just of the dance but of the music that accompanies it. The *pallavi* is not based on a story or song with lyrics like the *abhinaya*. It gradually unfolds the particular *raga* upon which it is based – forming a beautiful but challenging tapestry of rhythm, music and movement. *Megh pallavi* can be loosely translated to "rain dance" – a sweet and joyful choreography that elaborates on the rainy season. It is two years since that horrific monsoon accident had changed her life. She wants to pay homage to the rains. The things that break us also turn us stronger.

Any classical dance show ends with the Moksha – salvation. The concluding item symbolizes the release of the human life experience, and integration of the soul with God. Moksha signifies the surrender of the dancer to God. A pure dance sequence in fast tempo performed to the accompaniment of rhythms played on the *mardala* – the primary percussion instrument in Odissi. She is not part of this group performance – the rhythm is too fast for her to keep up. But she is not disheartened. She remembers her teacher's words – one does not need to move swiftly or elaborately to dance. She will be one among the audience for this one – praying for universal well being and harmony. Praying that dance will always be her life – on stage or off stage.

# 29

# TIME HEALS ALL WOUNDS

NICOLE NIELSON

It Doesn't. People heal wounds. And, people don't heal until wounds are treated.

Without treatment, wounds get infected; infections become septic, and suddenly....... you're gone.

I was 14. The school intercom called my name and suddenly I was with a social worker. My eyes avoided my undemonstrative mother and silent sister who had long since moved from home. I intuitively knew why I was there. I lay silent while it happened years prior and things I had witnessed had stolen my sleep since. That day it was no longer a secret within our large & religious family but made *explicit* to me that it was never to be spoken of again, to anyone. I went back to life an altered version of myself: without family or friends, and alone. I purged for the first time that day. It was an automatic response, as though my body needed to rid itself of a poison. Yet, food would become my best friend. It had given me comfort in the past and now it would numb my pain, my deep loneliness, and allow hours to escape the constant hell in my head.

Trauma and neglect would be the gateway to the mental illness that would hold me hostage for three decades.

As a child, I had big, deep thoughts. I was inquisitive, smart, sensitive, kind and extremely empathetic of both people and animals. What did they need to feel happy? I carried such a heavy weight that I don't recall ever having a carefree day. I wanted to understand the why's of everything and everybody, as well as understand my religion in light of the predator. I wanted to talk to God, receive answers, and understand the path to happiness. Although it was the 80's and having serious conversations, was not the norm, I wanted them. Continuously, I had one sided conversations in my head with the people I wanted so badly to talk to.

As a developing teen, the multiplying family secrets, lies and trauma compromised my ability to understand how to form genuine friendships and non-abusive intimate relationships. Children are resilient but need to feel a sense of safety, support, trust and understanding from someone to do so. I didn't feel any of those things. I was terrified living in the same house as my father. I was terrified of the rides to town when he would expose me to conversations inappropriate for any child. My mother had pulled me into her side too deeply with all of the big stuff as well, and relied on me to be a sounding board during her understandable depression and forward. I was left without emotional support. I needed to take care of her, as well as my younger siblings as she worked through her grief in her room. I felt a huge sense of responsibility to them. I was in an isolated world, paralyzed and trying to be validated, cared for and to earn love. I didn't know how much more to do. I was there to listen. I was a straight A student, and I was competing and taking piano, piano history, theory and performance exams at a high level. I volunteered, as well as worked full time in the summers starting from 13 years old, and part time through the school year. I babysat and made dinner in the evenings and cleaned the house on Saturdays. I went to church daily. I *did* need perfection for me, but I did not need it from her. I needed to hear that everything would be ok and that I was loved and why.

I will forever be grateful to a teacher who knew something was so wrong; he tried so hard to reach out to me, but more importantly to my mom to let her know of his concerns. I was secretly listening on the other line and wanted to scream out, "Yes, it is all *so* bad!!!" But, the lies and secrets were more powerful than his love.

We moved to a new city my junior year of high school. My mom attended college, and I lost any connection to normalcy. The family dynamics ensured that no one was ever at my plays, public performances, competitions or public speaking forums in which I often won with standing ovations. I had a very emotional connection to music but couldn't get that type of connection from the people I loved *so* much. I felt betrayed by family and by the teachings of our religion. These teachings maintain that family is the only thing that matters. Paradoxically for me, not being able to count on anyone was the running theme in my life.

I am proud of what my mother accomplished in her life and I loved her *dearly*. I understand that she had her own pain, and I'm thankful for her dedication to my piano. But, my monumental efforts to show her what I needed at 14 remained unaddressed. My body was visibly and literally dying, and I was dying *for her*. "Read your scriptures, for it is there you will find all your answers. Pray and listen and repent." What did I have to repent for? I hadn't done anything wrong. I could feel her resentment towards me building. She would take cruel shots, name call and withhold conversations. I was ungrateful and hateful towards God. He was the only one who could help me. I was so was confused. I begged God for someone to see me and know what I needed. It wasn't working to ask for it. My faith, my prayers, my innocence...they were no more productive than the despair.

I was the epitome of a high functioning, ambitious, hard-working addict. I never slept and I kept up. I knew I wanted to be happy, so I pretended to be happy. And, of course, did enjoy moments of life with people. Once I moved to the city, I was surrounded by many who reached out to know me. They saw me as funny, talented, smart and fun; yet, I still felt like I had little to offer. I felt peripheral to everyone while keeping up with a stressful and strenuous daily regimen of people-pleasing. I was dedicated to work, my mom, siblings, friends, volunteer efforts, as well as kind men I couldn't trust or commit to longer than a night. I even tried to please men who would brutalize with me abuse, words and control. I spent hours and weekends playing and having sleepovers with nieces and nephews wanting to ensure they felt loved by me. I still felt like one of them and I wanted to know them. I wanted all people to feel loved by me. I wanted to be present, to hear, and to let others know I wouldn't carry judgement. I tried to validate feelings, be empathetic and supportive in situations. I wanted to be Christ-like. I *did* care. However, I also over-functioned for people because obviously.... I was unlovable if I didn't.

For years I had Oscar winning performances forcing toxic positivity on myself. I kept the secrets and lived from a place of fear. I excelled musically, academically and professionally. I was an actor. I was a fraud.

Bulimia hadn't made me more confident and anorexia wasn't making me more disciplined. It wasn't giving me more control, and it wasn't giving me conversations or love. It wasn't helping my brain to calm and allow me sleep or stop the nightmares in the moments I would drift. Over the years I became physically and emotionally drained from trying to do and be everything and rely on my addiction as a coping skill. As ER trips increased and the last veneer went in, I lived in fear I would die in my sleep and eventually hoped I would. I hated it all, but my mind kept me in a daily ritual of planning, finding and filling the empty spaces.

Plans for recovery started a million times on a million Mondays, with varying degrees and terms of success, much like my continued efforts to confront the issues of my past and have the difficult conversations. I would enter the process with prayer, hope and will power. So many times, I was 'all better!' Yet, the trauma responses ensued. Other kinds of disordered eating patterns still haunted me. The isolation and loneliness was undeniable. The family pain seeped into every part of daily existence. My weight fluctuated wildly, and I knew others were judging me on how well I was living. Most often their judgements were wrong. I *really* wanted to get better. Treatment options were few in Calgary, and I carefully set up my own plan and rehab at a centre in the United States. When my family rejected the pleas for family sessions, I was hit once again with the realization that I didn't fit the right image, but harder yet was for me to feel love in action. Rehab didn't work. Many years in, I was starting to know all the lingo, I understood the therapy, I felt way too smart for addiction and I felt embarrassed. And yet, thousands of days were shaped by a dedication to disordered eating, and serving others, but never serving myself.

Through childhood, I had a genetic immune deficiency that resulted in constant chronic infections. The nutritional deficiencies I brought on in my early teenage years were accompanied by years of sleepless nights, and a serious car accident that left me with significant neck problems, migraines, shingles, poor dental work and other extraneous factors. I would suffer excruciating long-term facial neuralgia, terrifying A-typical perry Romberg syndrome as instigated by the neuralgia, worsening migraines, several exhausting autoimmune conditions, and palatal myoclonus. Then came the devastating loss of my new career that I had been so happy to have found.

My biggest fear came true. It was difficult to explain how I hurt. I couldn't explain my emotional hurt as a child, and I couldn't do it now with physical pain either. I felt silenced and alone both physically and emotionally. The toll it would take to hear that my sins had brought this on destroyed me again, and what I needed most was always withheld. Presence. Love. Support. Conversations. I knew they felt I was lying when it was *always* worse than what I would show. I felt homesick for a place I didn't know. I wanted to be where there was a possibility of feeling safe, loved, and a part of the family. This would become my bottom and lead to my suicide attempt. It was the only option I felt I had in leaving *all of the kinds* of pain.

Without ceremony or pomp and circumstance, one day I just stopped purging. I can't remember the day or date, which is so unlike me! But, disordered eating takes many faces. And, it took me much longer to find the freedom I was dying to know. My brain would often tell me it was just too late to find peace, freedom, healing and love. The truth was that I *really* had nothing. I could never truly be free; I would never have the kind of relationships I wanted with those I loved most. I did have a counsellor who was finally able to take me through the interwoven complexities of my life, loss and lead me to closure without the resolution I wanted. We worked on boundaries, and moving away from situations and people that hurt so deeply. It is difficult to heal in the places you became sick.

Has recovery from so much been linear? No. I still have thoughts I must acknowledge and wash away. Was it comfortable? Literally, no. Not one bit. I was physically uncomfortable leaving food, and I felt panicked *all* of the time. Could I learn satiety or intuitive eating if I'd never experienced it? What would I do besides pace the kitchen with my new time?

Through recovery, I figured it out. The emergence of my own *personal* spirituality commenced along with newly found self-compassion and creativity. I was able to use this in order to engage with recovery and connect to the world. This is how I changed my life. Finding yoga as well people I felt safe with to discuss eating disorders was significant. I began to let go of that secret and then another and another. I was still not comfortable believing anyone would like me, complete with my flaws, gifts, constant physical pain, and all. Real connections have been the most difficult. But, it is in shattering secrets and difficult conversations that we are seen. It took empathy and unfamiliar emotional maturity to become thankful for who I am. Today, I continue to learn how to find places in which I feel trust, and safety. I appreciate those that celebrate all the parts of me, and I continue to do what I can to reconnect and connect with family and friends in a way that is real, raw and beautiful.

I haven't purged in years, and I love and enjoy food now without many added thoughts. I so still grieve for that young girl that I was. I want to hold her and tell her all the things that I love about her *already*. I want her to know how much beauty she has in her old soul, and how much her story matters and will matter. I grieve years of missing genuine trustworthy friendships and building memories with people. I grieve not having children and not finding a partner who truly loves and respects me. But mostly, I grieve that the adolescent I was didn't have the opportunity to feel at peace in the world and with people. She didn't have the chance to love her body. A body made to laugh, move, love others and accept love *from* others. Currently, in the life chapter I'm in, I am so grateful. I am grateful *to my voice for finding me freedom, to my body for finding a way to stay, and to my mind to make it all meaningful.* My purpose no longer comes from that which is external, it is a part of my soul and I get excited to share it every single day. I am not and never was my trauma or chronic pain. *I am so many things.*

I couldn't have guessed what the implications would be of what I had done that day in the school bathroom. I was just trying to survive. My trauma responses were not Satan, like I was taught. What I endured was not a personal issue. It wasn't an issue with my sins or lack of repentance. *Nor* was my way out supposed to be thinking positively and letting go. The problem was trauma. The problem was secrets. The problem was shame. The problem was neglect. The problem was lack of conversations and connection.

Survival is meant to be a phase, not a life sentence. Contrary to popular opinion, *things can ALWAYS get worse. Time doesn't heal, but people can, and the time will always be now.*

# 30

# FINDING MYSELF

ANDREA HEYES

Knitting has always been my therapy...

No matter where I am or what I am doing, there is always a ball of wool and a pair of knitting needles in close range.

My Mom taught me to knit as a very young child and I can more or less still remember knitting my first jersey at the age of six roughly, on a circular needle with her assistance. Knitting is my happy place!

In 2019 I completed my first 67 minutes for Mandela Day project. This consisted of knitting 67 little lung warmers for newborn babies. A friend that matriculated with me had her husband's family over for a braai/BBQ and we were invited to join them. Her sister and mother in-law were both busy knitting one-piece vests for the Friends of Tambo Babies. I thought that this was too precious and decided to do the same. It took me most of two years to finish my little creations, and I still remember that in February 2019 I had twelve little waistcoats going at various stages of completion. Because I was so close to finished, I became overwhelmed and just couldn't wait to finish all 67.

A week or two after proudly handing in my first lot of 67, the lady from Friends of Tambo gave me a shopping bag with a few balls of almost antique chunky wool in it, and asked whether I would be interested in knitting booties?

Challenge accepted. I took off with my new little project, looking for patterns and figuring out how to make these little fiddly jobs called bootees. No sooner than a year later, 67 little pairs of booties were packaged in recycled sushi and cake containers ready to be delivered to the Friends of Tambo Babies.

2020 found me also completing 67 little beanies, just in time for World Preemie Day, November 17th. I handed this little project in to the founder of Beanies4Babies about two weeks before the hand-out date and I am already well on my way with the next batch for 2021.

It has taken most of eight years to get to where I am today. Through the processes of recycling, repurposing, up-cycling, thrifting, shifting, sifting and most prominently stretching rands as far as they can possibly be stretched, I'm truly finding myself.

At 42 years of age, I refer to myself as a semi-retired self-sustaining stay at home Mom, (SAHM) and there is absolutely nothing I want for. The realization of where I am at and all that I have, which is still materialistically way too much, is more than enough for me.

I run my handful of small businesses peacefully from home. In 2019 I finally got myself into gear and had a wendy house constructed, under my gigantic avocado tree in the forgotten corner of my garden. Wendy houses are usually built from thin narrow wooden planks which require annual treatment. This is now my sewing den. I have spent many luxurious hours in this glorious space creating all sorts of things I never thought I could.

Recently, we have been experiencing more load-shedding than usual in South Africa. This is when the power stations are struggling to keep up with the electricity demand and they switch areas off in Johannesburg for four hours at a time so as to assist with the recovery of the power station. I gifted my wendy house with its own solar panel, a battery, and an inverter. I can now sew happily, even when there is no electricity.

My love for sewing was suddenly re-kindled about two years ago when I dug through my pile of goodies, that were waiting to be repaired in my sewing box, and I found the oven gloves that I was given as part of my kit when I started my career in the Food Service Industry as a student 23 years ago. The corduroy at the back of these handy mittens had stripped due to being used and washed a lot. I decided that since I had a damaged pair of corduroy trousers that had gotten stuck and torn by my bicycle chain, that it was time to combine the two and sort this mess out finally.

No sooner I was on yet another mission. I drew a pattern and figured out what these oven gloves were made from. Now, my assistant and I make a few pairs of 'hotties' once a month which get sold through word of mouth, social media and randomly in pop-up gift shops. The initial idea of this little business was to create an empowerment project for unemployed women. Which, to a degree, has worked out; but, it will still require a lot more time and effort and resources to turn it into a fully fledged stand-alone successful entity.

My very dear friend asked me to make her a Shwe Shwe (a popular South African fabric) numnah/saddle pad for her birthday this year. At first it was quite a daunting project, but I accepted it gladly. Quilting the batting between two pieces of fabric still is not something I have mastered, however this project turned into three different numnahs for her of various sizes and qualities. I made and gave these to her over a few months. They were mostly made with African fabric. In her initial request, she included leopard print, and as a result it is a line of goodies I wish to pursue more intently. The world of horses really seems to be bigger than I ever imagined, now that I have done more research into the sport.

I collaborate with another friend to create the cutest little country dresses. She crochets the cotton bodices and straps, and provides all the nitty grittys for the completion of the dresses. I then get the most precious job of putting these gorgeous little creations together!

The last few years have been rather an emotional journey, dealing with my Dad's passing. He was a man I deeply adored, and this left a huge void in my life because there was absolutely nothing he did not provide for me. If I squeaked, he acted, and it has taken me years to get over being so super spoiled. Unfortunately, I was left on earth with a wicked step-mother. This was another rather large wave to ride but I did it, and it came to an abrupt halt a couple of months ago when she repatriated back to Germany. Once she was gone, a huge weight lifted off of my shoulders; one I did not realize was actually weighing me down as heavily as it did.

Finding my internal happiness has been the marvellous outcome of all the discipline and searching that I've invested into over the last few years. When I realized that the majority of our country is living on so little a month, and feeding many mouths, I realized I needed to look deeply within myself. Having been entrepreneurial since opening my very first business 20 years ago, I've had many advantages such as learning about business and how to do things cost-effectively. I can now operate frugally. My speciality is running a business with zero, or super low overhead.

Along my journey, a small miracle also somehow occurred, leaving me to feel like the most privileged person in this entire universe. I got to meet my true soul-mate. Since that encounter, literally everything just fell into place. It seems like everything that I was pursuing and tackling, suddenly and very simply all made sense. Initially I encountered a completely broken person, but almost three years later, a complete transformation is evident. Despite all of his hurt and turmoil, I discovered a truly awesome human being hiding away from all that life and people had thrown at him. He had no money in the world, no business, and no high profile job. There were no fancy dinners, but nothing can describe the complete honour of being able to have such an amazing connection with another human being here on planet earth.

As part of my process of minimalization and spending less, I made the decision that I would no longer allow myself to buy wool. This has worked really well to a degree, as even though I have mostly been knitting away at the wool stash accumulated over 30 years, there is still a bit of wool that remains. I also decided to stop knitting because I felt that I was spending too much time on it, and not enough time on things that were more productive. This worked well for a week or three, and I did manage to get over the withdrawal by distracting myself with other activities and things that needed to be done. Regardless, something was missing. I just did not feel complete. Something was lacking, and draining me.

The following week I went to spend some time with my soul-mate, and there is a really awesome fabric shop quite close to his part of the world. Since I had not bought the really lovely fabrics for oven gloves from this shop in more than a year, I thought it would be a nice treat. They also have a wool section, and I managed to get away with just one ball of dusty, light purple, chunky wool for the beanies, and have been selectively knitting very slowly one beanie at a time. The choice in colour comes from the colours around preemie day being grey, white and purple.

This was the final little box that needed ticking in terms of me knowing who the true me totally is. Yes, I probably do have a knitting addiction, but what has become clear, is that knitting has proven to be the only way that all of my stitches get held together. So, it is as if I am a huge ball of wool, and the process of knitting loops together is the story of me and who I am.

# 31

# THE PURSUIT OF SUCCESS

RIMA KACHALIA

While writing this, I shudder divulging the lessons I have learned in life up to this date. While climbing ladders hoping to achieve my goals, I have experienced dozens of ups and downs. I have felt like a trespasser and overcome hurdles to arrive in this moment. Here I am writing about my journey to become an academic. It has taken me 25 years to get to this place.

I begin with a question to myself as well as to those who underestimated me by believing that I couldn't and wouldn't achieve great things.

Can a person find themselves if they have struggled since childhood?

Or is it a futile pursuit to even try, because some things are just unachievable for some people?

The seven letters of the word S-U-C-C-E-S-S defined what I wanted to achieve, but I believed deep in my soul that I was not cut out for educational pursuits. Through childhood, I had always been a below average student at best.

Let's fast-forward now 15 years to high school. I simply could not wrap my head around Physics, Chemistry, Biology, History,

Geography or English. Math I and Math II were particularly challenging. But I tried hard both day and night and endured ruminating thoughts of failure that kept me awake.

In the presence of my parents I experienced anhedonia; I could not feel pleasure. Come grade ten, I finally passed with average marks. My parent's encouragement was relentless, and they would repeat to me with hope in their eyes that no matter what, I was going to ace my tests. Their words were my only source of motivation, and because of them I was able to accomplish passing grades. I'll never forget the day my parents received my tenth -grade report card. The marks were very low, but I passed.

It is indeed true that parents are true blessings. Instead of insisting that I explain my poor results, they continued to encourage me to move forward and believe that life could be beautiful. I remember that day so well, and reflect on how blessed I felt to have such encouraging parents that continued to show faith in me. They truly believed that I could accomplish big things. It was because of their undying encouragement that I began to gain more interest in academics.

In grade twelve, I finally scored well above average and was able to enter an excellent university. At this point I had two career options and decided to delve into banking.

By striving hard and having luck on my side, I achieved a Master's degree with a specialization in marketing. It took great courage and determination to get there. I often felt like a trespasser because I didn't always believe I should be there. It was truly incredible that I was.

Eventually I went on to complete a Master of Business Administration (MBA). Eventually the day came that people who originally underestimated me started asking for recommendations and seeking my advice about education.

My message to each and every person struggling is that when you fall down, get back up and learn from it. Start walking, one step at a time. If you do this, one day you will start running and eventually you will achieve your goals.

# 32

# NO DREAM IS EVER SILLY

DANIELLE MEADES

Why is it that in movies, main characters will wake up with a sudden awareness of who they are, as if someone has pulled back a curtain to reveal their true destiny and how to get it? The character then chases this destiny no matter the cost, against improbable odds, and with brilliant success as the reward. We may even know people in real life who have followed similar trajectories. For 30 years I operated under the misguided conviction that renouncing a lifestyle or swimming against the current were the only ways to find yourself. But *ah-ha* moments do not have to be so loud. My own, in fact, were a series of quiet discoveries, each building on the last, until they had formed a mountain so immense that I could not ignore it.

I wanted to become a published author.

Let me backup and provide some context. I knew I wanted to be a writer from a very young age. I had notebooks, binders, and floppy disks full of my stories and poems, and the times I spent writing were invigorating. I daydreamed about writing romance novels for a living and bringing joy to people's lives with my happily ever afters. Except, I had grown up surrounded by adults run down by their work, who were chasing promotions they didn't want and living for weekends and vacations. Didn't this mean that true happiness and careers did not co-exist? Writing brought me so much joy that by this logic, it could never sustain me as more than a hobby. Thus, like an obedient cog in society's wheel, I got a degree in health science, then a degree in nursing, and began my career as an RN. With this career came benefits, a stable income, enrollment in a pension plan, job security, vacation time and sick days. I received accolades from friends and family for the noble and difficult job I was doing. They patted me on the back for choosing the safe route that would let me enjoy my life after the age of 65.

I was miserable.

The funny thing about misery is that unless it is obvious, it's easy to slip into the belief that how you feel is *just being an adult*. I found a job offering autonomy and ample learning opportunities with the added benefit of wonderful coworkers. I picked up concepts and skills with ease, worked hard, and was good at what I did. Sure, there was no genuine joy, but wasn't this what the adults in my life had prepared me for? Friends in similar situations started talking about homes, cars, renovations, savings plans, and travel as they established their careers. There were so many goals I was instructed to have, and they all demanded money. Lots of money. As a nurse, I was making lots of money. I could have all the items listed above and be indistinguishable from everyone else. How would I ever justify leaving my superior full-time job just to chase a silly dream with no guarantee of financial security? Nobody else was doing it.

Here's the thing. No dream is ever silly. Let me repeat that. No dream is ever silly. How would I justify leaving my job? I couldn't, and so I didn't. But I wasn't passionate or happy and lacked the understanding that I didn't *need* to justify quitting. Being good at something and enjoying something are *not* the same thing, and that is a hard lesson to learn. If you are not passionate about what you do for multiple waking hours a day, you are floating through life with no real purpose and *that is not okay*. If you have a nagging sense that you were meant for something different, don't ignore it. This defined my first quiet discovery: the things everyone else seemed to crave and work toward did not fulfill me or bring me joy.

In 2016 I had my first child, and while on maternity leave, I started writing again after a several year hiatus. One day, my husband studied me and said, "Have you noticed how much happier you are after a writing session? I've never seen you this giddy after a nursing shift. In fact, I don't think I realized how unhappy you were until now." I was dumbfounded and prepared to argue, but he was right. I hadn't been happy. I love music, but if I am glum, stressed or anxious, I do not want to hear a single note, and it had been six years of very little music in my life. This is no longer the case on the days I make time to write or work on my dream. I am playful. I have patience and capacity for my family. I feel excitement and wonder. And I pair some great tunes with some not-so-great dance moves. For six years I allowed writing to get crammed into the back of a trunk, dusty and neglected, instead of traveling in the front seat and shouting out directions. This was my second quiet discovery: whether it takes days or years to realize how miserable you have become, the response will be the same. Find what sets your soul on fire, hold on to it for dear life, and start doing the work.

The first part of my work involved steps that were wildly outside of my comfort zone. I joined the Romance Writers of America, a non-profit association, and found my local chapter, the Toronto Romance Writers. I attended conferences and seminars. I acquired the domains for websites I wished to use. I discovered books about writing and found local writers to meet with at coffee shops and libraries. I started an Instagram account and joined Facebook groups. I took part in NaNoWriMo. I joined a critique group. I kept writing. And here's the huge one: *I let other people read what I wrote.* I spent 30 years hiding my passion from the world. Over the last four years I have opened the tap on sharing it, at first as a drip, then as a trickle, and now as a steady stream.

But society's indoctrination of how success and progress are measured remained rooted deep inside me, and it scared me. My family was proud to inform people I was a nurse; would they be as proud to disclose that I was a romance author? My son was in Montessori, and I wanted him to learn the skills of skating, swimming and skiing. We had a second son and started outgrowing our small home. Our car was old. So I kept nursing. As I type this right now, I am on my second mat leave, and still employed as an RN, because it took me four more years of quiet discoveries to shed the last layers of indoctrination. My mountain's structure was not complete until this past September.

In late August, after trying months of a pandemic, lockdowns, and a newborn, one of my best friends died while 30 weeks pregnant.

The tragic passing of my friend was a quiet discovery. A nurse practitioner, she owned two homes, travelled, wed, and had pets; her way of life fit into society's narrow definition of success. What puts a smile on my face when I think of her now? The memories we shared, and the knowledge that she always went after what she wanted. That's it. The rest doesn't matter.

I understand that after an unexpected death, it is natural to engage in a thorough study of your own mortality and question all the decisions you are making. Most people complete this exercise, but as the months pass and the grief changes, they restore their previous way of life. That was not the case for me. Enough quiet discoveries had developed before my friend's passing that the situation only fueled a fire that had been steadily growing beneath me since 2016. I suspect this is why her death was not a vulgar, punch in the gut kind of revelation. I enrolled in a course on the Coursera website called *The Science of Well-Being* by Dr. Laurie Santos of Yale University. During the course, she reported on studies that established that once an individual was making $75,000 USD annually, their happiness no longer increased with a raise in salary. We all assume that if we push hard and make more money and buy that next best thing then we might finally be happy, but it is *scientifically proven* that this is not the case.

Here I arrived at another quiet discovery. If being a nurse and striving to earn $100,000 a year would not increase my happiness, and the work to achieve that target made me miserable anyway, what if I altered my thinking once and for all? What if I built a life where I got to enjoy working? What if my children got to see a happier version of me? What if I quit struggling to please other people and focused on myself instead? What if I stopped caring about owning or getting what everyone else had, because things and stuff don't matter? What if I created a life so wonderful that the words retirement and vacation no longer existed in my vocabulary, because I would not require a break from what I was doing? What if my cup was so full of happiness that I could pour into the cups of everyone around me, improving the world I'm leaving my children? What if I could manage all that *without* changing my life in a way that would negatively affect my children and husband?

I stated before that my mountain became so tall that it was impossible to ignore, but that's not accurate. I think the mountain was always there, composed of all the hardships I have experienced and the compromises that have displaced me from my path. Every time I stayed faithful to myself or faced a fear, I advanced closer to the peak. In September 2020, I reached the summit and for the first time my vision stretched for miles, unobstructed and beautiful. I stood on the shoulders of the lessons life has taught me and understood that finding yourself does not have to happen as one giant moment in your life. It can be all the little moments along the way. There is a saying my husband and I quote to each other often that we heard on an episode of the Tim Ferriss Show: "Easy choices, hard life. Hard choices, easy life." Finding myself has involved making hard choices, no matter how insignificant they may seem. This means I will go back to work as an RN when my maternity leave is over, but in a reduced capacity. I will chase my passion to construct a more authentic life, at the cost of not affording the things that never made me happy in the first place. I will work as an RN just enough to pay my bills and keep my children safe and happy. I have drifted away from society's expectations and it is exhilarating to stand on my own. Life is long, or life is short. Tomorrow is never promised. It is up to us to be who we desire to be with the precious time we have on this earth. I will put in the work, make my hard choices, and trust that one day soon I will transition into a full-time career as an author.

Pay attention to your own quiet discoveries that push you up your mountain. Make your hard choices. Give your energy to your passion. Never stop working on what fills you with the most zest for life, even if it takes you the rest of your years. Live a life celebrated for being joyous and authentic.

Start today. I promise it will be worth it.

# SHE WAS HERE ALL ALONG
DAWNA GRIFFIN

*To begin this journey of finding myself we need to start at the ending. I blossomed into the beautiful, strong, creative, inspiring, dedicated woman I am. I just wish I realized sooner that she was here all along; she just needed to be brave and let the world truly see her.*

I was born and raised in a small town on the East Coast of Canada. As a child I lived a simple life. You could find me spending my weekends in the country, walking dirt roads or picking blueberries. I had dance parties to S Club 7 with my cousins and was confident in who I was. It wasn't until my favorite person in the entire world, my maternal Grandmother (Nanny as we called her) passed away suddenly, that things didn't feel so "simple" anymore, and my confidence began to shatter.

Losing someone close to you in your pre-teen years is deeply impactful. During a time in life where you are trying to work through every feeling, and emotionally charged hormonal moment, losing someone means that you have one less fan in the stands. One less person who *sees* you for who you truly are and loves you for that. One less monumental person in your life to remind you that you are worthy just as you are.

The road from that pivotal moment on was a hard one. I would spend the majority of my teenage, and young adult years trying desperately to fit in. Lost in understanding who I truly was, I shape shifted and formed myself into someone I thought I needed to be in order to fit in with those I associated with. I hated who I was and who I was becoming, yet I continued to live that way. Looking back at those years, I can still feel the pure loneliness. I wish I could time travel back and save younger Dawna from the heartbreak she would feel and her dangerous coping skills. Coping skills that included a vicious cycle of numbing with drugs and alcohol accompanied by pure neglect of body and soul. I had no clear path as to where I was going. I had no idea who I was. I was lost. It wasn't until I got pregnant with my daughter that I had my "ah-ha" moment. This was my sign from the universe that said, "You're worth more than the life you are living."

Whatever higher power you believe in, I thank them. I thank them every day for the miracle I was given in a seven pound, nine ounce blue-eyed baby girl. She saved me in every sense of the world, and in a full circle moment I named my miracle after my Nanny, beautiful Stella.

I wish I could say that when I walked out of the hospital, the sun shined down on me and everything made sense from there on out. Wouldn't that be so easy? That didn't happen, but Stella was a start. She was a start to a ten year journey of unlocking who I truly was and allowing her to be seen.

Breaking unhealthy cycles isn't for the faint of heart. Letting others see your deepest, darkest moments or thoughts takes guts. Admitting that you need to make changes to better yourself takes vulnerability and courage and I applaud anyone who has done it in their life. To this day I am still in therapy working through my various traumas, and it's gut wrenching at times. If you are reading this, keep going. It's not easy, but it's worth it.

As I began to release myself from the chains of my shame and guilt that held inner me locked away, the world started to feel different. Incorporating healthier coping mechanisms into my life allowed me to see myself with fresh eyes. I am worthy, I matter, and I have all along.

Throughout my journey I eventually found the courage to share my pain, struggles, happiness and successes with others. And, in turn, I began to find my voice. A voice that started out quietly in the back, and then began to grow into a loud roar. A roar so loud that people didn't always appreciate it. With my newly found roar I needed to navigate how to not let other's opinions silence me. Not everyone is going to love you, but that doesn't mean you change who you are for them. Your voice matters. It needs to be heard. You need to be heard.

After years of soul searching, I have come to learn that I am meant to uplift and inspire others. I am meant to share parts of myself to help someone else feel less alone and bring people together through common experiences. I now can appreciate the pain I experienced because it built me into someone who can show empathy and care for others in similar situations. I am a care-giver by nature and want to make everyone feel loved and remind them of their worth. This is who I am.

If someone told 15-year-old Dawna where she would be right now, she would laugh. I can hear her now: "Yeah right! There is no way you are on some 'online platform' where thousands of people can see you screaming from the rooftops about body positivity, sharing your pain, or promoting others to love themselves. There is no way you are hosting events and getting in front of crowds of people. Girl, not you. You don't even like people looking at you!"

She would also likely have so many questions about what Instagram was and what I meant by a 'hashtag.' Oh, I reflect on the simpler times before social media, when a hashtag was the pound key. Period.

Looking back on my journey, I am thankful for every tear, heartbreak, experience, and moment of growth. Above all else, I am thankful for that one single moment in time where the universe reminded me of the miracle that this life of ours is. Our life is precious and our time on this earth is never guaranteed. May we all love each other harder, speak kinder to ourselves, chase our dreams, and never let another person silence our roars.

*Dedicated to my beautiful, strong, inspiring Nanny, Stella Griffin. My #1 fan. Whom I've come to realize, has been in the stands all along.*

## ABOUT THE AUTHORS

**Sangria Sisters**

If there's one word to describe the sisters, it's fun. Val MacLean and Lori McGillivray share how life isn't always rosé behind the white picket fence in their hilarious humour blog "Sangria Sisters." Relatable and real, they tackle titillating topics with trucker mouth care. The Sisters use their platform to champion women and causes close to their heart. Their goal is to spread kindness and joy every damn day.

Join the sisterhood at www.sangriasisters.ca, the Gram @sangriasistersblog, Facebook @SangriaSisters, and Twitter @sangria_sisters

**Shelby Watt**

Shelby Watt is a field safety advisor for an oilfield construction company in central Alberta. She grew up in Ponoka, but The Hen Den (cabin in Sylvan Lake) is where she and her cat, Cat, call *home*. She indulges in massive dirty chai's and loves to sing in the shower. In her free time, she can be found taking long walks on the beach, reading in the hammock, and/or contemplating the universe (and her place in it) with friends. In the past year, Shelby has taken up journaling as a daily practice and enjoys sharing snippets of her thoughts, poetry, and photography online. You can find her at @shlebylynn (personal) or @shelms.realm (poetry) on Instagram.

### Mae Kroeis

Mae Kroeis has always been passionate about supporting others in being mentally healthy and living life to the fullest. She has a Master's Degree in Public Health in Health Promotion with a Bachelor of Arts in Psychology and has worked for over 15 years in community mental health promotion. As a Certified Professional Coach with Maek it Happen Life Coaching, she helps people who feel stuck at work or in life figure out what they are really meant to be doing with their lives and go for it. In addition to helping others pursue their passions, Mae loves playing hide and seek with her kids, telling bedtime stories and exploring Calgary's parks and mountains with her family. Mae is also a published freelance writer and an Applied Suicide Intervention Skills Training (ASIST) trainer. You can find her on Instagram @maeking_it_happen or on her website www.maekithappen.ca

### Tanya Bast

Tanya Bast is a Personal Fitness Trainer, former fitness competitor, wine connoisseur, mom, and a women always seeking new entrepreneurial adventures. She was born and raised in a small town in Alberta. She now resides in Vancouver, BC. Traveling several countries and life experience has helped fill her tool belt with many stories for her to share. She hopes to write and share more of her life adventures. You can find Tanya on Instagram @tanyabast_tftraining

### Philippa Kaye

Philippa was born and raised in Yorkshire and completed her degree in London before heading to the mountains where she worked six ski seasons in Austria, France and Canada. Following that she spent several years working for luxury tour operators in London, discovering India, Sri Lanka and Nepal. She is a traveller, writer, adventurer and self-confessed Indophile. She has spent thirteen years living in and traveling extensively throughout India, writing about her experiences periodically for Times of India, Travel Mint and regularly on her blog www.memsahibinindia.com. She has ridden priceless Marwari horses, been invited to royal weddings, threatened by the local mafia, trekked mountains, rafted white-water, been wined and dined by maharajas, drunk chai in remote villages, slept out under the stars, driven vintage cars and got caught up in Holi, ending up with her hair dyed a permanent shade of green.

What all of this taught her, was that there is so much more to India (Sri Lanka and Nepal) than meets the eye, and more than what is generally sold by travel agents. Therefore, during her thirteen years in India, she set up Indian Experiences as a consultancy to the Indian Travel Trade, running product training sessions, developing websites, content writing as well as developing marketing campaigns and social media strategies to help the industry promote what she calls, 'The Real India.' She is also the author of Escape to India, a novel based loosely around her travel adventures in India.

### Pixie Wright

Pixie Wright is a classically trained dance artist and accomplished fine arts educator. She calls Alberta home, but is fortunate to travel internationally in her role as a dance examiner. Pixie may be highly trained in expression through movement, but she has loved creative writing for as long as she can remember. Once upon a time, Pixie's communication skills intersected with her natural sense of justice and she found herself in law school. That was fun. Now, Pixie is happily settled as a mom, fine arts specialist teacher, dance examiner and story teller. She is incredibly grateful for any platform to promote authenticity, courage and heroism. Pixie is highly anticipating the upcoming release of her fictional autobiographical series The Pixie Chronicles. You can find her on Instagram @pixie.communications and on Facebook @pixielandcommunications

**Veronica Buccinfuso**

Veronica is dedicated to creating connections with women and entrepreneurs to build a supportive community focused on fun and well-being as director of the Airdrie, Alberta branch of Wine, Women & Well-Being. She has built and sold two previous businesses, and now uses her hands to create beautiful and happy homes with the transformative power of organization and decorating. As owner of Happy Place Spaces, she is continuously learning about design, organization and feng shui principles. She loves all things that help us be our best self and hopes to pass on her love for meditation, yoga and acoustic guitar onto her two children, Jaxson and Madi.

You can find Veronica on Instagram at @happyplacespaces and @winewomenwellbeingairdrie, and through her website: www.happyplacespaces.com

**Holly Jones**

A lover of life, fashion, cooking, baking, wine, health and all things 'people'. She is married to her perfect person with two grown children and proud to carry the title of "Nei Nei" for two tiny humans that complete her world.

Along with being a wife and mother, she has spent 40 years in a Nursing career, specializing in Critical Care to Geriatrics, caring and providing compassion and giving to others.

Adopted in British Columbia Canada, from a Ukrainian, Indigenous and French heritage, she spent most of her life on the East Coast until very recently leaving behind all she knew and loved, to embark on an adventure. Never too young, 'they' say. Think big, follow your dreams, inspire, create, grow, be authentic and embrace a life of change and ongoing learning –

So very blessed. You can find her Holly on Instagram @Holly-jeanjones24 and on Facebook at Holly Jones

**Abisola Olapeju**

Olapeju is the author of the upcoming book, *Unbox Your Purpose* and founder of the MindDiet Company, a service-based organization focused on helping women build kick-ass confidence to navigate from confusion to clarity of purpose with a goal to live out her best life. Abisola is a Pharmacist with passion in women's mental health and a certified project manager who has deployed her strategic skills to help scale multinational brands in Africa. She was born and raised in Nigeria but currently resides in Canada with her family. She is a life-long learner, running a certification in interpersonal psychotherapy and loves adventures, listening to music, dancing and travelling. You can find her on Instagram @coachpeju or her website www.minddiet.ca

**Tish Wallis**

Tish Wallis is a stay-at-home mom to two energetic boys, a mobile massage therapist and an independent consultant with Arbonne International. Born in the Okanagan and raised in Ontario and Alberta, she is very happy to call Calgary home.

Through her journey of personal growth and self-development, she is finding ways to break down labels and use her voice within to inspire others to say yes to the things that make them happy.

This creative mom has a love for plant based health and wellness, ballroom dancing, crafting and travel. You can follow her and her journey on Instagram @happyathomeceo.

**Theresa Stadnyk**

Theresa grew up on a mixed grain and cattle farm in Southern Alberta, a few miles away from the UNESCO site of Writing-On-Stone Provincial Park. She left the farm for Calgary, Alberta, where she graduated from SAIT Polytechnic in the

Engineering Design & Drafting Technology program. She ended up later instructing at the same technical college. She now has her own company and contracts as a Sr. Civil Engineering Technician. She has designed numerous subdivisions, campgrounds, storm ponds, parking lots, transportation designs, open pit mine development and reclamation, site drainage, stream diversions, river engineering, underground utility design, site grading, erosion and sediment control (ESC) and heavy civil construction.

She has a love of art and you'll find her sketching, water painting, acrylic painting and now exploring digital art. She's known for her smile, being loud, and loving a good chat. She enjoys making memories, is always up for adventure and travelling with her three boys and husband.

### Aisha Akram

Aisha Akram is a 19-year-old student, who is currently studying for a Psychology degree at university, in hope of a career in the field of mental health. She was born and raised in Manchester, England and has lived there for her whole life. She is very passionate about social issues and raising awareness for topics that are considered taboo in society, such as mental health, feminism, abuse, injustice, racism and many more. Her love for writing inspired her to start an Instagram page dedicated to her poetry/prose, which allows her to express her emotions freely and make sure that other people know that they aren't alone in their struggles. As a young South Asian girl, she is aiming to contribute to the de-stigmatization of mental health problems and reminding women that their voices hold so much power in them, despite what society may tell them. You can find her on Instagram @aisha.akramx where she often posts stories that address social issues or via @a.writes, where she posts her original writing in the form of poetry or prose.

### Kelsie Chernenko

As one of three sisters, Kelsie is a classic middle child: she is the family peacekeeper, has an easy-going temperament, and is generally level-headed (unless you ask her husband).

Kelsie has always wanted to be a mom so she eagerly anticipated the birth of her son as a fulfilling life experience. Instead, Kelsie had an identity crisis, which propelled her down a path of self-discovery. To get through this crisis, Kelsie took to writing as a form of processing what she was going through, navigating her new identity as a mom, and reclaiming her ambition. Pen to paper, she rediscovered her voice, one word at a time.

On her path, Kelsie uncovered a passion for coaching. As a coach, she utilizes her motherhood experience and background in Human Resources to help career-driven newbie moms who feel unfulfilled by motherhood, wanting to pursue their professional ambition. She believes that as moms, we can have it all: a badass career, a happy family, and space for ourselves as individuals.

When she's not chasing a toddler around, working her corporate 9-5, or coaching moms, you can find her at the local café savouring a hot cup of coffee and listening to jazz. You can find Kelsey on Instagram @kelsiejanecoaching and her website www.kelsiejanecoaching.com

### Lindsay Amyotte

Lindsay Amyotte is a 36 year old mother of 2 school aged children. She lives in Sherwood Park, Alberta. Lindsay is a preschool teacher, and loves her job. Lindsay is a first-time author and very excited to be a part of this project!

### Melissa Pasutto

Melissa is a master teacher and taught elementary school for 33 years. She believed in leading an environment whereby her children were supported to learn and grow to their fullest potential academically, as well as in their intellectual development.

Including as well, their social and emotional well- being. She was an advocate for children and took an enthusiastic approach to engaging and challenging her students to push past their preconceived limitations and realize their gifts and talents. Teaching was her passion, and her mission was to stretch the thinking of young students, teach problem solving and build resiliency.

During Melissa's career as an educator, she earned many accolades which included the prestigious Loran Scholar Award for teachers building future leaders in the community which is recognized by the Governor General of Canada. Melissa was also the recipient of numerous Pan Canadian Student Choice Awards, Excellence in Teaching Awards spanning over her years of teaching with the Calgary Catholic school district. One of her most rewarding roles as an educator was as a liaison and a facilitator for Catholic Community of Caring since the inception of the program. This role involved her planning, organizing and presenting monthly assemblies to the student body of about 500 students on average, including parents and colleagues, with a platform focus of values, virtues and morals.

Melissa is a mother of two, a wife, motivator and mentor to many.

### Joy Laughren

Joy Laughren is a Canadian prairie girl with a penchant for all things creative. She left the corporate world where she was a technical writer and software trainer for eight years, to chase around her two adorable little girls. Nowadays she spends most of her time cooking nutritious recipes to be reviewed and tested by her family. She shares the real-life hits and misses as a food blogger with Leave it to Joy. You'll also find her freelance ghost writing for small businesses specializing in empowerment, honesty and reality.

She also enjoys creating handmade celebration decor as the

entrepreneur of Birthday Box. Birthday Box was developed as a creative outlet that offered affordable personalized décor to aspiring Pinterest Moms.

Keep up with Joy online at leaveittojoy.wordpress.com and Instagram at @birthdaybox.yxe and @leaveittojoy

**Allison Silvaggio**

Allison Silvaggio has been in the travel industry since 1997. She has travelled to all seven continents and realized her passion for writing while travel blogging, www.greatcanadiantravel.com/author/allison/. Allison has been practicing yoga for over 15 years and has now completed her 200-Hour Online Certification. Her choice to study yoga has much to do with the world of travel and exploring new places & cultures. She believes in learning by experience and choosing your own path to happiness.

Allison and her husband Mark have been married since 2004, and have a blast with their two son's, Nicholas 15, and Liam 12. Together they enjoy travelling, spending time at the cabin, along with activities such as golf and hiking.

Life has slowed down over this past year, which has allowed Allison to have more time for reading, writing, and enjoying a nice glass of wine. Next year she hopes to return to Nashville, as she lives for country music!

You can find her on Instagram @allie_b13.

**Lisa Webb**

Lisa Webb is an educator, author, speaker and entrepreneur. She used her experiences as a global citizen living abroad as an inspiration to to share the power of community with others; creating *Wine, Women & Well-Being*, a place to connect women and build community. Under the Boutique Press, *Canadian Expat Mom*, Lisa has created a platform for women around the world to share their stories by publishing the anthologies *Once Upon an Expat, Life on the Move*, and now

the six books in this series, *Her Voice*. She also champions
women by sharing their stories on her podcast, *May Contain
Wine*.

You can find Lisa on Instagram wearing many hats,
@lisawebbofficial, @winewomenwellbeing and @maycontain-
winepodcast.

**Martina Pinto**

Martina Pinto is a Marketing Communication Manager and
a self taught Visual Artist. She resides in Mumbai, India with
her family. While she pursues business writing as a part of her
current profile, she also shares a profound passion for painting
and photography. She believes in the power of positivity and
inner strength which she depicts in everything she does.

Martina loves to write poetry, some of which have been
published in local journals. She also likes to travel and pen
learnings from her escapades. She is very fond of animals and
loves to stay in tune with nature, as she believes that it
strengthens the human spirit. She has been recognized by the
World Art Branding Conclave for her paintings and many of her
photographs have been featured in corporate calendars.

You can find her on Instagram @pintomartina and on Facebook @MartinaPintoArtist

**Cecile Dash**

Cecile Dash was born in The Netherlands, married a Canadian backpacker that she found in London and is a mom of
three beautiful little monsters (oops meant to write children).

Taking care of others is her second nature and when giving
up her professional career and moving from The Netherlands to
Congo, this was something she applied wherever she went.
Falling in love with Congo and its people made it even harder to
leave after five years.

She then moved to the Middle East. Dubai's contrast to
Congo-life was extreme #fromjungletodesert. Thinking her

family was used to a hot climate after five years in Africa, she nearly melted during her first Middle Eastern summer.

After two years in the desert, it was time to try out the best part of North America... Canada! (Molson says it so it must be true!) Going from 7seven years in flip-flops to temperatures of -40 was something that took some adjusting. Good news! Cecile survived the extremely harsh winter in Canada and is currently trying to establish a life in the beautiful Canadian Rockies.

Despite the moves and changes of scenery, Cecile has continued to advocate and fundraise for those in need and is a humanitarian at heart.

Cecile has been previously published in numerous anthologies like; *Knocked up Abroad Again*, *Once Upon an Expat*, *Life on the Move* and *Extraordinary Experiences, Tales of Special Needs Abroad* and if she ever finds the courage, she will publish her first children's book which has been ready for quite some time now.

### Tonia De Sa

Tonia De Sa is a woman with many hats: mother, teacher, healer, friend, daughter, sister, entrepreneur, and now, writer. She loves bringing people together in community whether that is in an elementary classroom, a group of girlfriends or her Facebook Blog, *Thrive with Tonia*.

Tonia has lived in Calgary, Alberta since the age of 2 calling herself Canadian first but also having roots in Goa and East Africa.

She lives a full life with her teenagers either ignoring her or sharing their funny antics with her. They are surrounded by a village of good people that keeps evolving. She keeps pushing herself to dream so that they can follow their own heart's bliss as well.

Tonia has always loved writing since she was a little girl writing plays, poetry and stories. She was first told she would become an author, by her beloved Grade 10 English teacher, when she turned in a story to him that was 239 pages long inspired by a long-time crush.

Tonia put aside writing for many years besides keeping a journal and creating books for her loved ones. She still turned to writing for expressing herself and keeping a record of her life.

In the last half of 2020, writing became a means to channel pain and wisdom. Tonia took a deep breath of courage and shared her vulnerability in her *Thrive with Tonia* group so that others would know they were not alone and that there were ways to find their inner light.

She is thrilled to be published in the Her Voice anthology as an important step on the path to her dreams.

**Amy Lynn**

Amy Lynn is a teacher by day who lives in Edmonton, AB with her husband and puppy. She loves listening to music while sipping a cocktail in her woman cave. Her life mission is to create the perfect dinner party playlist. She can be found roaming around in the Rocky Mountains during her time off from work. You can also find her on Instagram @mi_ami_lin.

**Stephanie Knowler**

Stephanie Knowler (she/her/hers) is an avid coffee drinker by day and wine enthusiast by night. Stephanie holds a BA, BEd., and an MA in Educational Research. A former elementary educator, she is now the Dance School Director & Owner of Evolutions School of Dance, a successful dance studio entering its 15th year of operations, in Calgary, Alberta. Stephanie takes great pride in her success and growth as an entrepreneur and leader in dance education, but also in her ability to combine her love of early childhood education and learning with her passion for dance as a career.

In her "spare time" Stephanie can be found chasing after her 4 kiddos - all 8.5 and under. This is her first experience being a published writer - hopefully the first of many!

### Sharana Ali

Sharana Ali, owner and Founder of BOSS The Six Edition; a collective empowering individuals (particularly those self-identifying as female) to refine and define their full potential through brunch opportunities and a support system.

Sharana is a divorcee and single mother to a strong willed, confident, firecracker who she knows will one day change the world.

By day, Sharana is taking over corporate Toronto, and by night she is THE BOSS. Eating, sleeping, and seeping every ounce of glory from this amazing city she calls home. She is a rosé-all-day supporter, takes her coffee double, double and as dark as the roast can get.

Through BOSS Sharana is on a mission to dispel the idea that we need to be on this journey of life alone. Together, through sharing our experiences and stories we can unite in our emotions. No topic is off the table; if they say it's taboo ...Sharana says let's bring it to the table.

Find Sharana on Instagram @Bossthesixedition

### Danielle Thompson

Danielle is a mom of two medical miracles, a Disney lover, and a healer through and through. She is always teaching herself and evolving to better serve her purpose on this planet. Danielle finds her peace behind the steering wheel of a race car; as she drove on dirt tracks for over 8 years. Nowadays, she finds peace in meditations and writing. Just as her hobbies are wide spread, so is her professional path. Danielle is the owner of Beautiful Balance - Energetic Healing & Education. Her mission is to empower and heal women of this realm with energy work, self discovery, mindfulness, meditation, colour therapy, reflexology, self care and more. Find her on Instagram @daniellebeautifulbalance, on her Facebook Group Beautiful Balance

Community or her website www.beautiful-balance.
vistaprintdigital.com

### Samantha Tufts

Samantha Tufts is a recent Public Relations graduate and
lifestyle blogger from Ontario, Canada. Outside of work, she is a
writer, creator and wannabe author who dreams of being a
"New York Times Bestselling Author" before the age of thirty. In
her blog, *Merci*, she writes about her passion for skincare,
personal development and fitness. You can always find her reading, writing, working out or trying to learn something new. Find
Samantha on Instagram at @mercibysam or on her personal
blog mercibysam.blog

### Renata Pavrey

Renata Pavrey is a nutritionist by profession, with a BSc and
an MSc in Food Science, Nutrition and Dietetics from the
University of Mumbai. She is also a certified Diabetes Educator
from the International Diabetes Federation, and has done her
Pilates teacher training from Michael King Pilates, UK. She is a
trained Odissi dancer under the tutelage of Smt. Asha Nambiar
from Vaishnovi Kala Kshetra, a marathon runner, a dabbler in
the arts, with a penchant for learning languages.

Books form a large part of her life and reading and writing have
been lifelong hobbies. She reads across genres and languages,
from authors around the world, and her writing spans from prose
to poetry on dance, sport, movies, and animals. Her poems, essays,
reviews, and stories on a myriad of topics are featured on her blog
*Curious Cat*. Her venture *Tomes and Tales* is dedicated to all things
bookish – from discussing books to interviewing authors, making
crafts and cooking food inspired from books – in keeping with her
belief that books have stories within them and around them, and
we create our own stories with every book we read.

You can find her @tomes_and_tales and @pilates_positivity_with_ren on Instagram, and at www.tomesandtales365.wordpress.com.

## Nicole Nielson

Nicole lives in Calgary, Alberta, and is a writer sharing some things she always meant to say, but didn't. She plans to use her new passion of the written and spoken word to reach, inspire, and empower children and teens struggling with addiction. Nicole grew up dedicated to the piano, singing, and doing school drama and outside of having a corporate career, used these talents to pursue voice acting and singing.

A learned extrovert and natural introvert, she is passionate about social justice and equality, volunteer work, teen issues and above all, her nieces and nephews. Nicole loves to travel and while her current visit is invariably her new favorite place in the world, will always move towards the music. She loves west end shows, her birthday season, religiously watching basketball and fears the stairs of unfinished basements.

## Andrea Heyes

Andrea Heyes, holds a National Diploma (N.Dip) in Food Service Management, from Technikon Witwatersrand which is now University of Johannesburg.

Andrea lives in Kensington, a town in Johannesburg, the economic hub of the Gauteng Province, South Africa. Born at the historic Marymount Maternity Hospital in Kensington and raised and schooled in Edenvale not too far away by an Austrian Mother and a German Father. Her writing journey is only just beginning, she journals often and is in the process of compiling/authoring '67 Reflections...' inspired by her 67 projects for Mandela Day, the side-effects of technology and her amazing teenage daughter.

You can find her on Instagram @thenymphecottage, Facebook @thenymphecottage and LinkedIN as Andrea Heyes.

## Rima Dhruv

Rima is a lecturer by profession and writing is a skillset hobby of her. She was born and brought up in India, living in Mumbai with her family. Her passion is travelling, eating various cuisines, watching movies and writing. As a lecturer she loves to interact with children and tries to learn something from them. You can find her on Instagram @rima839.

### Danielle Meades

Danielle is a registered nurse with degrees in health science and nursing, but her most important job is being a mom to two energetic little boys (and one energetic husband). For the last three years she and her family have been living in Orillia, Ontario, Canada and loving the community they have discovered. In her spare time, Danielle enjoys tackling DIY projects, spending time in nature, travelling, and having stimulating conversations about life, mental health and the future. She dabbles in plant-based eating, meditation and workouts that make her curse. While Danielle is proud to work in healthcare, her true passion is writing and she is working toward becoming a published romance author. You can follow her on instagram @author_dmeades or find out more about her at www.daniellemeades.com.

### Dawna Griffin

Dawna is full-time educational assistant by day who has developed a love for writing in her spare time. She also owns a photography business and has a passion for creating memories through the lens for her family and clients. She was born and raised on the beautiful Prince Edward Island, and considers the ocean her happy place. Dawna decided to trade ocean views for mountaintops and now resides in Alberta, Canada with her family. She is very passionate about sharing her journey to self-love, experiences in motherhood, and the road she is on to working through her childhood traumas. She calls herself a 'Hype Girl' and takes pride in building up the woman around her while encouraging them to find their voices in this world. You can find her on Instagram at @dawnadoiron.

## ABOUT THE EDITORS

### Marcey Heschel

Marcey Heschel is a Canadian author and mental health therapist. She holds both a Bachelor's and Master's degree in Arts, and currently lives in Houston, Texas with her husband and two young children. As expatriates, her family has enjoyed living abroad, seeing the world, and learning about new cultures. Marcey has published three children's books that discuss mental health related topics such as empathy, anxiety, and mindfulness. She has also been published in three anthologies related to expatriate life.

As the In House Mental Health Therapist and Book Club Director for Wine, Women & Well-Being, she works to inspire and connect women through her passion for self-development. Her greatest pleasure in editing the "Her Voice" anthology series has been witnessing the courage of the contributors. Marcey comments: "Through vulnerability and shared experience, these women will unknowingly help each other; and, that's a beautiful thing."

In her spare time, Marcey can be found water sliding with her kids, training for half marathons or scuba diving shipwrecks.

Follow her on Instagram @marceyheschelwellness

More about her children's books: www.marceyheschel.com

**Lisa Webb**

Lisa is a teacher, author and heart-centred entrepreneur, who uses her Masters in Educational Leadership to guide women towards becoming the best version of themselves.

Having lived on four different continents with her family,

Lisa raises her two daughters as global citizens, documenting some of their many travels through her children's book series, *The Kids Who Travel the World*.

Writing under her pen name, *Canadian Expat Mom*, Lisa has given a platform to women abroad to share their stories through the anthologies *Once Upon an Expat* and *Life on the Move*.

She is the Founder of Wine, Women & Well-Being and host of the podcast, May Contain Wine. Lisa feels passionately about building communities that support and uplift women.

Manufactured by Amazon.ca
Bolton, ON